THE CHASE
AND RUINS

THE CHASE
AND RUINS

ZORA NEALE
HURSTON
IN HONDURAS

SHARONY
GREEN

Johns Hopkins University Press—Baltimore

Johns Hopkins University Press
2715 North Charles Street
Baltimore, Maryland 21218
www.press.jhu.edu

Library of Congress Cataloging-in-Publication Data

Names: Green, Sharony Andrews, author.
Title: The chase and ruins : Zora Neale Hurston in Honduras /
Sharony Green.
Description: Baltimore : Johns Hopkins University Press, 2023. | Includes
bibliographical references and index.
Identifiers: LCCN 2022038714 | ISBN 9781421446660 (hardcover ; acid-free
paper) | ISBN 9781421446677 (ebook)
Subjects: LCSH: Hurston, Zora Neale—Travel—Honduras. | Honduras—
Description and travel.
Classification: LCC PS3515.U789 Z696 2023 | DDC 813/.52—dc23/
eng/20230302
LC record available at https://lccn.loc.gov/2022038714

A catalog record for this book is available from the British Library.

*Special discounts are available for bulk purchases of this book. For more
information, please contact Special Sales at specialsales@jh.edu.*

To my parents, Garcia and Estella Andrews,
Zora, and the ancestors in and beyond
the state of Florida, the US South,
and the Caribbean Rim.

Your presence is felt.

Your protection is appreciated.

I came across her after she was gone.

Dear Science and Other Stories
Katherine McKittrick, scholar

———————————

Except for the waters of the Gulf being a most
godly blue, the voyage was uneventful.

Zora Neale Hurston, literary genius, 1947

———————————

One comes back and there's
no dog gaily wagging its tail for us.
(Uno vuelve y no hay perro que
alegre su cola por nosotros.)

"Memorial," Rigoberto Paredes, Honduran poet

———————————

can't even get close to nobody no more . . .

"My Sweet Lord / Today Is a Killer," 1972
words by George Harrison, David Nelson
with improvisation by singer Nina Simone

CONTENTS

PREFACE

*On Selective Remembering and
Hurston's Chase "Down There"*

Most people who are aware of Zora Neale Hurston's legacy do not know that she visited Honduras in 1947, staying eight months. While there, she wrote a book that many of her fans bypass. In it, she did not focus on people of African descent, as she had in prior writings. There were concerns about her writing abilities and motives. A false accusation in 1948 that nearly drove her to suicide also figures into the silences of this decade, as does her being more politically conservative than most folks living in her lifetime and ones living today care to discuss. All of these issues figure into why the 1940s are often overlooked. More emphasis is placed on the 1950s. Perhaps this is because she began her final decade working briefly as a maid.[1]

The news headlines concerning immigrants from Central America—among them, the ones placed in the detention centers that week Texas froze over—led to my interest in the 1940s, or the decade following her heyday in Harlem.[2] "Winter in Gaza. / Babies freeze to death. / Soldiers shoot children, / aiming for their eyes. / Light a candle for us all," Alice Walker has written, pointing to the despair felt worldwide.[3] A poem, even a beautiful one, told me so much. I received larger context for this kind of suffering. I would learn more via Hurston. Along the way, I'd learn more about a very complicated woman.

But how to tell this story? I tell the story carefully because of the sparse evidence and the sorrow already surrounding her later years. Katherine McKittrick has talked about the twitch-iness of the past and how we don't always have evidence for the assertions we make.[4] Hurston left behind just twelve let-ters concerning her visit to Central America. She wrote them in Honduras while looking for a Mayan ruin. She joined other visitors, including adventurers, businessmen, tourists, and researchers who sometimes romanticized Latin and Carib-bean America. But Robert Hemenway, Valerie Boyd, Vir-ginia Moylan, and other scholars have addressed in varying degrees how complicated Hurston has been on this front and others.[5] So are the people who chronicle her life. Our "par-ticular way of remembering" her may resemble the selective forgetfulness of powerful nations when they tell the stories about the ones they claim to save.[6] At least this is the analogy that one scholar, Patricia Stuelke, has suggested by linking the growing interest in restoring Hurston's legacy in the 1980s to influential countries boasting about efforts to rescue their piti-ful and once colonized brethren at that moment. The States' encounters with Grenada, a tiny Caribbean nation, is but one of many examples.

Whenever a savior emerges, there are bound to be prob-lems, though. Certainly, the initial drafts of *Seraph on the Suwanee*, Hurston's seventh and final novel, which she wrote in Honduras, positioned her as having an inside-outsider view of the US South.[7] She also claimed to have an advan-tage over white academics while studying the Mayans.[8] Such researchers were not Brown, which is to say, from a margin-alized group like her, so they missed things. She could claim her Americanness on the one hand and her Blackness on the other, although doing either south of the border was risky. *Ser-aph* was neglected by later Hurston critics and fans alike, and she never found the ruin. In 1960, the 69-year-old two-time Guggenheim winner died broke.

She seems to have first visited Honduras in 1930 after fall-ing out with Langston Hughes, another core member of the rich explosion in intellectual and artistic output of the 1920s and 1930s Harlem Renaissance. The once-close friends had, in fact, collaborated on *Mule Bone*, a play based on her life. But Hughes wanted to credit the typist who had been assisting them on the project. Hurston balked at this suggestion and, unbeknownst to him, filed the copyright in her name. When he discovered as much, their friendship was never the same.

After this incident, she headed to the Bahamas and continued on to the very place she would sit in 1947: Puerto Cortés, a port town on Honduras's northwest coast. If you tilt your head while looking at a map, the water curves there, forming lips on the land. Mexico City is a 23-hour drive away, and if you keep driving—not walking—another 33 hours, you could be in Los Angeles.

The 1930 trip was little more than a reconnaissance mission. She stayed three months. At the time, she told Ruth Benedict, a professor at Columbia, about a mystery city in the mountains on the Mosquito Coast, near Nicaragua.[9] It was not until 1947, after her most productive years in Harlem, that she made it back to Central America, a region cupped on the north by Mexico. To the west and the south is the Pacific Ocean. The Caribbean Sea and Colombia swoop down to the east, hemming in Honduras, Panama, Costa Rica, Nicaragua, Guatemala, El Salvador, and Belize. For far too many, it is all simply somewhere "down there."

I was a sophomore at the University of Miami when I heard about the revolutions "down there."[10] An earthquake in El Salvador left more than 100,000 homeless in 1986. My sorority pledge club participated in a clothing drive. This was our way of helping the faceless.

I had a friend who did more, Ollie Matheus. I met this aging man with a long, white beard in St. Louis in the mid-1990s. He told me about the days when he wanted to fight with the Chiapas in Mexico and take up arms with the Sandinistas.[11] He had already helped rebuild villages in Nicaragua after the clashes with rebels there. He had been an activist in Haiti, too, where he met Jean-Bertrand Aristide before the Catholic priest became his country's first democratically elected president. All those places felt "down there," unlike the Florida peninsula, my home state. My people arrived in Miami from Mississippi, Georgia, and the Bahamas in the first half of the twentieth century. Some of them came from the Savannah Sound settlement in Eleuthera. Eleuthera means "free" in Greek; in that word was our destiny. We were among those chasing the warmth of other suns, as Isabel Wilkerson put it.[12] We were the people Hurston studied. So were her own people. Her family fled white hostility in Alabama to Eatonville, the country's first all-Black township, shortly after she was born in 1891. There, freedpeople in the late nineteenth century bought 112 acres from Josiah Eaton, one of the few white men interested in seeing Black folks do well. The town was named for him.

In looking at the world around her, she saw the land and the things on it. She saw Lake Okeechobee, a body of water that sits like a belly button on the peninsula. I'd fished with my mama's kinfolk on this lake. I'd also held a map on my lap as my grandparents took backroads to get there from Miami. I was the navigator, calling out the names of the towns ahead long before we entered them.

After graduating from UM, I became a reporter for the *Miami Herald*. During this time, I wrote a story on the first festival held in Hurston's honor in Eatonville. While there, I interviewed her goddaughter Harriet Moseley.[13]

The ties between Hurston and me go beyond our upbringing in Florida and our both being writers. I was 53 when I sat down to write this story. Hurston was 53 years old when she went down to Honduras in 1947. There's more. Hurston passed away on January 28, seven years before I was born on this very day. She died in Ft. Pierce, a couple of hours north of the city where I came into this world. I have been to her grave and other places she visited, including the white sands of Daytona Beach, the city where she lived on the Halifax River when she decided to return to Honduras.

This book argues that the complicated Hurston many of us see sought the location of a Mayan ruin in an attempt to stay fed while experiencing a decline in her writing career. At the time, she also invited readers to think about a particular idea: before the conquistadors arrived and before all of the talk about who was white and who was Black, there was sometimes joy on this side of the Atlantic Ocean. In escaping to one of the places where Indigenous people had sometimes thrived before contact with Europeans and Africans, she experienced a bit of joy. She also made discoveries about herself evident in her surviving letters and how she shapes her protagonist in *Seraph*. Her ability to do both was partly tied to the way she sidestepped categories from time to time. In Central America, she was still Black. She was still a woman. But she was also American, a category that gave her a bit of social currency. Her time in Honduras speaks volumes about the great ironies of modernity. Down and out or not, she was a citizen in one of the most powerful countries in the world. Honduras gave her that.

CHAPTER ONE

AMID THE JEALOUSY AND POLITICS, SHE RUNS

Zora Neale Hurston had been humored and bothered even. The three señoras were at it.[1] They were making promiscuous love. That is how she remembered it. Unrestrained love. Promiscuous and unrestrained. She picked those words. There they were on the paper filling up with other words. She was in Central America with the others, their numbers growing. They all wanted something. The miners, businessmen, laborers, researchers, and tourists had all been down there after the fruit companies began making money. The soldiers were there, too. Hurston walked among them on her quest to find herself an ancient Mayan ruin. It was in Honduras, a country that, as she once put it, has "given me back myself."[2] This is what she once said about the place where she sat now.

Years earlier, she foretold her own presence there. In 1926, she sent a greeting card to Fannie Hurst, a white novelist who was one of the first people to help pave the way for her rise in Harlem.[3] The illustration on the card is an oracle pointing to the good and bad ahead for the still-young Hurston: a woman arching her back before a bright orange sunrise between mountain peaks. Honduras is filled with such mountain peaks.

Hurston never wanted to go to Central America alone. The Second World War was still on when she invited her friend Jane Belo, a white anthropologist, to come along. They had once compared the trances of people in Bali to the religious

Young Zora Neale Hurston sits in a white blouse with a dark scarf around her neck.

Photo A.5, Zora Neale Hurston Papers, Photographs Series A, Box 14, Folder 1, Manuscripts Collection, Special and Area Studies Collections, George A. Smathers Libraries, University of Florida, Gainesville, FL.

practices of Black folks in Holiness churches in South Carolina.[4] Finding a Mayan ruin required another pair of professional eyes, maybe several pairs. This discovery was the kind one would immediately share with a friend. "Jane, darling, I want you to join me," she told Belo about her wish to travel to Central America.[5] "I have never wanted to do ANYTHING so much.[6]

Carl Van Vechten also heard the excitement in Hurston's voice. With a camera and a pen, he helped document the Harlem Renaissance. Some saw him as little more than an interloper in a thriving African American artistic and intellectual scene.[7] "Nigger Heaven" is what he called the flourishing moment for mostly Black creatives and emblazoned on the cover of his 1926 novel.[8] Despite his brash language, Hurston seems to have found in him a confidante, if not a friend. "I wish that you could come along," he was now hearing her say. But he did not go. Neither did Belo.

To go south, she first needed to go north. From a pier in Mobile, Alabama, Hurston boarded a commercial ship for her journey to Honduras. She stepped down into Tela, a port on the north coast.[9] "Except for the waters of the Gulf being a most godly blue, the voyage was uneventful," she told Max Perkins, her editor at Scribner's, in May 1947.[10]

Within one month, Perkins would be dead. Burroughs Mitchell, his replacement, would take over. He'd get to hear all about her adventures in Honduras, formerly a Spanish colony. Nearby Belize had been called British Honduras, as the English controlled it until 1973. With such outcomes of empire hovering, she departed for Tegucigalpa, the country's capital, likely to let the government know she'd arrived. They'd all want to keep tabs on a distinguished writer but also an African American woman. Not even her ties to a powerful country would stop that. Blackness had long been associated with negativity.

It did not matter if she were welcomed by important people. Before her departure, she told one colleague that the family of Tiburcio Carías Andino, the country's president from 1933 to 1949, supported her expedition.[11] Whether she really knew the kinfolk of this statesman is unknown. She was by now acquainted with many people in high places, though. She once claimed to have even corresponded with Winston Churchill and Richard Nixon.[12]

After wandering a bit to get her bearings, Hurston decided to use Puerto Cortés, the port town on the far northwestern coast, as her base. There, she found a room in Hotel Cosenza.[13] At the time, rooms in the country cost between $2.50 and $5.00 a day. With meals, visitors might pay $5.00 to as much $10.00 per day.[14] Because she did not have funding, she needed to be mindful of all expenses. Given the gastrointestinal problems from which she suffered, she may have purchased packaged provisions to avoid raw vegetables and salads as well as to better manage her money. She purchased a mosquito net to fend off the malaria she'd suffered while visiting western Florida in 1942.[15] She could easily get it again in Puerto Cortés, a port city of about 8,000 that included Chinese and Middle Eastern immigrants and people of African and Spanish descent, as well as Indigenous people. Some of the latter lived the mountains.[16] One particular Indigenous group, the Miskitos, lived farther east and near the ruin she wanted to find.

Hurston wrote Perkins that Puerto Cortés had the most interesting people.[17] She mingled among people whose ancestors could be traced back to the Black Caribs, who themselves could trace their past to both the Amazons and the Africans. The latter had survived the wreckage of two slave ships in the mid-seventeenth century.[18] These Africans stalled any attempt to make St. Vincent, a British colony, a leading producer of sugar. After two wearying wars, a naval convoy relocated these belligerents west to the Bay Islands off the north coast of Honduras in 1797.[19] More than of half of the Caribs died en route. The rest migrated to the mainland.[20] Some either stayed on those islands or in Honduras; the rest left for Nicaragua, Guatemala, and Belize.[21] By the late nineteenth century, the Garifuna, the largest ethnic group of Black Caribs and the long-standing Black population in Honduras, warily watched Black West Indian laborers arrive in Honduras, looking for work.[22]

Hurston herself was looking for that Mayan ruin. First, she needed to write at least one draft of a novel to ensure the prospects of another check from her publisher to fund her expedition. While she settled in, she continued studying her surroundings and decided the obvious: Honduras did not have the money one could find in the United States.[23] Still, she liked it there partly because she did not see striking workers, communists, and other "sea-buzzards."[24] She especially had no use for communists. Liberals either. She believed they all used African Americans as pawns. She was a Republican after most Black folks in the States had crossed over to the Democrats. Henry Louis Gates Jr. has characterized her neither as a complete "Uncle Tom" nor as a radical.[25] She was, however, something. Langston Hughes, another Black Harlem Renaissance writer, certainly knew how Hurston could be loving. She could also be anything but.

She may not have known all the particulars and, when convenient, even turned her head from certain social conflict, including the matter concerning the prospering foreign fruit companies. Labor strikes began almost immediately, one as early as 1917. A new deal on wages and a US warship quieted the unrest for a while. Since its independence from Spain in 1821, Honduras was sorely challenged with internal fighting and outsiders.[26] It would have been worthwhile for any outsider to know the basics about the land, its past, and present, politically and socially. At the time of her visit, about 1 million people lived in a nation roughly the size of Tennessee or England. Three years before her arrival, a group of women led a protest outside the Presidential Palace in Tegucigalpa to secure the release of some political prisoners. That same year, exiles from El Salvador tried to topple the Honduran government. Like the United States, Honduras had a two-party system. The country's government, however, was historically unstable. Between 1824 and 1933, there were 117 presidents. Again, Hurston probably averted her eyes. She would refrain from involving herself in these issues.[27] To get involved might jeopardize her success, and, she told Mitchell, her new editor, she had no interest in any of it.[28] "Artistically, it is too trite to be taking a poke at the politics of Latin America," she said. It would be patronizing, in fact.[29]

She was quite aware of her ties to a more powerful country filled with people who looked down on most of its neighbors in the Western Hemisphere. This was the case even though keeping tabs on the often-smaller nations remained important to decision-makers in DC. This was not new. Not long after its own revolution against Great Britain, the United States looked south, asking Europeans to not establish new puppet governments on this side of the Atlantic.

As she attempted to steer clear of problems in a country with a historically trying political scene, Hurston strategized how to embark alone on her expedition. By now, she was often alone. This was not new either. She was at odds not only with Hughes but with some of her other Black male literary peers back home as well as some of the growing number of women conducting research outside of the United States. She certainly clashed with Benedict, her professor at Columbia. Benedict was an editor for the *Journal of American Folklore* when Hurston wrote an article in 1931 on voodoo in the United States for it.[30] It has been suggested that Benedict disliked African

American women and was threatened by Hurston's eccentricities.[31] Benedict, who eventually became the president of the American Anthropological Association and American Folklore Society, apparently once wrote an unflattering recommendation for one of Hurston's Guggenheim applications and even mailed the recommendation late.[32] Benedict may have been jealous of Hurston's creative approaches to academic writing. Benedict was also a poet, but she produced her work under a pen name to avoid sullying her professional image.

Some of the tensions between the two women involved Margaret Mead. Hurston was the first Black graduate at Barnard where Mead was one of ten bob-haired students nicknamed the Ash Can Cats. They both continued their scholarly training at Columbia where Mead worked with Benedict, who became her lover.[33] Mead's study on the sexual freedom of the Samoans later captured the public's imagination and pushed the boundaries of gender, race, and sexuality in academic research.[34] Without question, Mead and Benedict were the better-known women pioneers in anthropology. Evidently feeling jealous herself, Hurston once told Belo that if she came down to Honduras, they could make Mead's study on the Samoans "look like a report produced by the Women's Christian Temperance Union."[35] But Belo didn't come.

Perhaps like Hughes, Belo knew to be cautious with Hurston, who, when she wanted, distanced herself from others. She could even be dismissive of the cares of everyday people when she sidestepped politics in less established countries where she conducted research. In *Tell My Horse*, her 1938 book featuring the folklore she gathered in Haiti and Jamaica, she recalled the artistic skills of Edna Manley, wife of Jamaica's white statesman. Mrs. Manley's sculpture "belongs in New York, London and Paris," Hurston wrote, adding that the First Lady's art was being squandered in Kingston save any mention of it in the *West Indian Review*, "the voice of thinking

Jamaica."[36] She could have been deliberately provocative. This was almost certainly true when she mentioned the unrestrained love of the three señoras. She uttered their misdeeds to her editor, a white man.

*

When she wasn't listening to the three women, Hurston might have walked from time to time to the Ulua River, which she surely passed in Puerto Cortés. The river flowed down from the mountains, eventually spilling into the Gulf of Honduras on the east coast near the approximate location of the ruin she so desperately wanted to find. As she plotted her next move, she doubtless saw the hustle and bustle encasing her. The fruit steamers from New York, Bristol, and New Orleans all went to Tela, the port at which her own boat had docked. Ships passed through La Ceiba and Omoa, two other ports on the north coast. Like the railroads and roads built by the fruit companies, the docks were critical to the country's economy. Coffee is now the product most often to leave Honduras, but during her visit, bananas were the key export. Between 1947 and 1948, as many as 14,557,000 stems of bananas were shipped to the States.[37] Coconuts were sent north, too.

O. Henry, the acclaimed short story writer, went to Honduras in 1890. He bore witness to the frenzied coast and recorded his memories of it when he created Anchuria, a fictitious Honduras, in his 1904 *Cabbages and Kings.*[38] In this fabled country, police cut paths through thick grass with machetes. There were, however, roads and stone sidewalks running beside the adobe houses that disappeared when the palm-covered huts of the Caribs and other poor people come into view. The dilapidated cabins holding the Black West Indians came next.[39] No matter where people there resided, they lived in a "banana republic." O. Henry coined the term, still in circulation, to name foreign exploitation in this part of the world. Among the ones creating trouble were the corporations making money on bananas.[40] The corruption had gone on for centuries, so much so, the poor there barely knew who precisely to call "master."[41]

Christopher Columbus arrived in Costa Rica in 1502, ten years after landing in the Bahamas, thinking he was near India. He named it for what he sought: "rich coast."[42] Ferdinand, Columbus's second son, is said to have given thanks to God at the sight of Mayans in a canoe. His crew overtook the Indigenous people before them and seized everything of value.[43]

Some 3 million Indigenous people were in Honduras as the conquistadors began arriving in growing numbers by 1524. Countless armed rebellions commenced. Hernán Cortés, the conquistador who seized Mexico, looted and destroyed anything in his path. It is for him the town in which Hurston sat writing is named. When the Hondurans at last rid themselves of the Spanish in 1821, the chaos continued as president after president was ousted. The coffee oligarchs cleverly maneuvered for power, too. As they did, more outsiders poured in, hoping to obtain wealth, too.

O. Henry described the adventurous souls who wanted the ears of important officials.[44] These newcomers hustled along a main street beside a beach and next a broad way where stores, a post office, military barracks, rum shops, and the marketplace were located.[45] Meanwhile, sloops took fruit to the boats waiting offshore. From time to time, a strange-looking brig from Spain or a French sailing ship with three masts would hang around, worrying the customs house.[46] By morning, the stock of alcohol and dry goods in town was larger.[47] Funnier still is what happened when a telegram arrived: groups of women whose complexions ranged from the fairest olive to the most intense brown rushed to carry the message, probably a proposal for another railway that would never be built.[48]

The president's summer home was called the White House.[49] The connections to the home in which the US president lived could not be missed. Everyone wanted to be like the "Americans." This is what people in the United States are called even now. They had been so prominent internationally, they took the title even though people living elsewhere in the Americas could make a claim to it, too.

One young Honduran woman spent a considerable amount of time with the "Americans." She had gone to a convent school in New Orleans and could have passed for a girl from Norfolk or Manhattan.[50] However, she could also wear a native dress with billowing sleeves that showed off her bare shoulders.[51] Foreigners often considered women like her to be as exotic as other things that were presented on postcards.

The postcards showed the predictable: jungle scenes, native huts, and palm trees.[52] The progress that wealthier nations were attempting to bring by building roads, railroads, and bridges in this country was also highlighted on postcards. In the 1930s, attempts were made to improve the infrastructure of towns like La Ceiba. Besides postcards, the foreigners overseeing these projects brought home to their children books that parted the curtain on life in Honduras. Honduran author Hilda de Castañeda received letters from boys and girls all over the world curious about whether her people were all savages.[53] Her tiny book would dispel that myth, presenting them as cultured and smart people who built stately buildings, including churches and hospitals.[54] Some of these buildings appeared on a postcard printed in the early twentieth century that features a short block in La Ceiba, the town where, she bragged, O. Henry wrote *Cabbages and Kings*. The image appears to be taken before the workers and women awakened one morning. In the foreground is a man with dark skin. He wears a hat, a long-sleeve white shirt, and slightly baggy pants. He gives the impression of moving slowly. So much there moves slowly.

UNA CALLE EN LA CEIBA.

STREET, LA CEIBA, HONDURAS, C. A.   115169

Street, La Ceiba, Honduras, circa 1920s.
Curt Teich & Company. Courtesy of Newberry Library.

By the time Hurston arrived in 1947, the mail from Puerto Cortés was taken daily to Tegucigalpa, the country's capital, but mail sent to Amapala on the country's southern side traveled just three times a week.[55] Some delays were caused by the daily two-hour siesta locals took from their labor. Surely aware of the uneven distribution of wealth siphoned from the country, some Hondurans put off completing work until the next day, a practice known as the *mañana* syndrome.[56] Given the poverty, those naive enough to advance money will hear "mañana te pago" (tomorrow I will pay you).[57] The latter was tied to the creed: Don't leave for tomorrow what you can leave for the day after tomorrow. In truth, *mañana* may never come. Under such conditions, a researcher must be persistent.[58] As persistent as a mosquito—especially during fiesta days and national holidays when no locals will work.[59]

Hurston was swindled in such an environment. Shortly after her arrival and aware of her need to raise money—there would be mules and guides to hire when she traveled to the jungle—she began collecting material for freelance stories to sell to *Holiday* magazine.[60] For one month, she apparently remained so focused on this effort, she sent apologies to Van Vechten and his wife, Fania Marinoff, a Russian American actress, for not updating them on her progress.[61] In the same letter, she once more tried to get Van Vechten to join her in Honduras. She thought he might want to photograph Santa Rosa de Copán, a city 92 miles west of where she was staying. There, he could find an already discovered ruin. She really needed his talents for herself. Indeed, when she eventually visited Santa Rosa de Copán, she hired a photographer who cost her "plenty."[62] The photographs were either insufficient or never delivered; she told her editor "something went wrong somewhere."[63] The ordeal was so devastating, she needed money "for necessities," by which she likely meant food.[64]

Such suffering was minor when compared to the kind endured by others there who looked like her. By the 1940s, many of the descendants of the Black Caribs migrated of their own volition to the United States for better opportunities away from the fruit fields. During the independence movement that lasted from the 1820s through the 1870s, they served as soldiers, worked for lumber companies, and even smuggled before turning to the plantations. They saw West Indians coming to Honduras with the skills to work in both the fields and on the railroads being built by the fruit companies anxious to efficiently get their products onto waiting ships.[65]

The West Indians, not the Black Caribs, who are known today as the Garifuna, were the ones picked for the labor gangs in Puerto Cortés, Barrios, Tela, and La Ceiba. However, both groups were reliant on the foreigners and collectively worried about their ability to earn money. By 1950, the poorest there still earned no more than $15–$20 a month.[66] A live-in housekeeper could expect no more than $1.50–$3.00 a

DEPÓSITO DE CAOBA CERCA DE LA CEIBA.

A MAHOGANY DUMP, NEAR LA CEIBA, HONDURAS, C. A.   118166

A mahogany dump near La Ceiba, Honduras, circa 1920s.
Curt Teich and Company. Courtesy of Newberry Library.

MAZAPAN, LA CEIBA, HONDURAS, C. A.   118167

Mazapan, La Ceiba, Honduras, circa 1920s.
Curt Teich and Company. Courtesy of Newberry Library.

week.[67] Skilled and industrial workers, however, could make $3.00 per day.

Not unlike some of the country's less fortunate people, Hurston skillfully maneuvered during her stay in this country. Again, as an African American researcher, she believed that she had some advantages over foreigners who were white, a race to which she could also make claim given her own white ancestry. Her paternal grandfather Alfred Hurston of Loachapoka, Alabama, near Auburn, is, after all, listed as a "mulatto" in a US Census. That said, she declared in one essay, "I am colored."[68] Still, Hurston boasted, "Frankly, they say that they would prefer me to a 'Gringo' who would come down. . . . I am just as sure that I am going to make history as I . . . am black."[69] She embraced her African ancestry even now as she, again, believed that part of her background set her apart from otherwise well-positioned white researchers. This part of herself gave her a connection to the Central American people, who often relied on their spirituality and not just the scientific. "Being what they call here a Mestizo, (Mixed blood) I am getting hold of some signs and symbols through the advantage of blood," she told her editor about the ones who were of mixed race, too.[70] She even declared, "Being a mixed-blood will be in my favor. The President himself is part Negro."[71] Most accounts of Andino's life hardly situate him in the way that Hurston had. His racial identity could be as vague as anyone else who was partly of African descent. No matter what, her biggest asset was her US citizenship. When intoxicated Nicaraguan soldiers brutally beat an African American military officer in Puerto Cortés in 1907, a white US commander said the Nicaraguans would face murder charges should the Black man, who was from Louisiana, die.[72] Racial lynchings were on the rise in the States, but African American soldiers were still US citizens who were evidently sometimes worth protecting.

This murder occurred in a country where whiteness was still most prized and so much so, *mestizaje*, or the practice of deemphasizing one's "Blackness" and "Indianness" was common.[73] On paper, many Hondurans made other declarations, too, though. In 1910, as many as 61.1 percent of Honduras said they were *ladinos*, or people of Spanish and Indigenous descent. As many as 16.2 percent of the people self-identified as being *indios*, or Indigenous outright. Some 9.6 percent were Mestizos, or mixed race. Five percent were *blancos*, or white. Just 3.4 percent were considered *negros*, or Black, and 3.3 percent were mulatto, or people with Black and white ancestors. Finally, 1.3 percent were *amarillos*, or Asian. These ways of seeing existed as more white foreigners arrived.[74]

*

Some people headed inland, as did one Missouri family arriving in Honduras in 1957.[75] John Blumenschein, a white physician, loaded up a Volkswagen bus with his wife, Marian, and their five children. He planned to build a home and open a clinic in La Suiza, an isolated valley that was typical of Honduras.[76] Situated southwest of Lake Yojoa, in northwest Central Honduras, La Suiza is Spanish for Little Switzerland.

For three months, the Blumenscheins took whatever wretched roads they could find to get there.[77] Upon their arrival, John left his family to buy their land.[78] While he was away, Marian and the children decorated a rented building with what they'd brought along, even using the seats from their Volkswagen bus for furniture.

Not long after they settled in, Marian was relaxing on the veranda and saw a little dog passing. She discovered that he had crawled through a small wall in the kitchen and taken a five-pound sack of flour. A caretaker at a resort for the United Fruit Company helped her chase the dog. This dark-skinned, scraggly man, who wore shoes but no socks, finally caught the dog and returned her the flour.[79] "Oh, no, it's yours," she said, only to see the man "without further ceremony" walk away.[80] The flour belonged to him, not to someone so used to having food that she would carelessly secure it.

The Blumenscheins tolerated their monotonous diet of rice and beans and pancakes made of flour, water, baking powder, and on one occasion, eggs,[81] and they soon owned one-eighth of a 4,000-acre estate at the south end of the lake that drained into several streams.[82] There, a team of researchers from Tulane University and Denmark had walked in 1935.[83] They reported vegetation in neighboring foothills so dense, it was nearly impenetrable. This very feature had attracted the Mayans, whose possessions were discovered, among other places, in the soil beside the lake.

Finding such artifacts became trickier the more one traveled away from the northern coast where the fruit companies had built roads, rail lines, and bridges.[84] As late as the early 1940s, Tegucigalpa, the country's capital, was several miles from a highway. Although the 1914 opening of the Panama Canal further revolutionized the movement of people and goods in the Western Hemisphere, and airports were built in Tegucigalpa and San Pedro Sula by the mid-twentieth century, transportation problems in the country could be expected. While there were all-weather roads that were passable during the dry season, anyone trying to cross rivers, valleys, mountains, and inaccessible areas like rainforests would have needed a mule, as was common in Central America.[85]

Dust on Her Tongue, a collection of short stories by Guatemalan writer Rodrigo Rey Rosa, cannot be told without consideration of the transportation challenges that are so threaded throughout his book (and Central America), they almost become a separate narrative. In one story, a Guatemalan man returning home sees how his city has grown. He feels the plane in which he is riding banking and curving in a sunny

THE CHASE AND RUINS

sky.[86] The plane lands, hitting potholes on the runaway. As he leaves the airport, the sounds of guitars and drums along the waterfront offer up a city that is sometimes disconnected from time.[87] Another story is set in Guatemala after the Second World War. By now, a station wagon is able to carry a load of wood to the other side of a river via a road that has only of late opened up.[88] The Blumenscheins saw many poor roads, one so narrow and muddy, it took an hour to go just eleven miles. The deep ruts left by the lumber trucks were just that destructive.[89]

The location of Blumenschein's home had only recently become accessible by car after a road was built during the Second World War. Before then, motor vehicles had to be ferried five miles across the lake. Like the Guatemalan towns that Rosa beautifully captures, these are the white man's roads.[90] On some of them, one can see a stream of lights, "two streams, one red and one white."[91] The roads exist alongside the sounds of the Old World, including Garifuna funeral chants.[92] Anyone hearing such chants probably coped, too, with the presence of monkeys, jaguars, iguanas, armadillo, deer, coyotes, and other wildlife.[93]

The stunning landscape offered consolation for any visitor's frustrations. As was true on the Mosquito Coast near Nicaragua, the mountains in northwest-central Honduras rise sharply. Aside from such beauty, the Blumenscheins counted other blessings: the United Fruit resort invited them to swim in the company's pool.

*

No matter her advantages as a US citizen, Hurston probably never received an invitation to swim at the resort owned by the United Fruit Company. By the time the Blumenscheins came to Honduras in 1957, Emmett Till had been dead two years in a country where some of its citizens tried for decades now to show off the promises of democracy. She heard such promises but remained focused on the work before her. Columbia University's Franz Boas, the distinguished German and father of modern anthropology, had taught her how to manage in such difficult environments. Her willingness to master this skill was evident in Miami in 1929 when she was reviewing her notes from her fieldwork on folk religion and witch doctors in the nearby Bahamas. Demonstrating the extent to which she knew how to steady herself while studying sensitive subjects, she told Boas via letter, "I hope that you will have time to read the material soon," adding, "I have tried to be as exact as possible. . . . I shall not let myself creep in unconsciously."[94] She likely reminded herself of this very thing while watching, perhaps from her hotel window, a group of *norteamericanos* building a storage tank for Texaco near her hotel.[95]

If the people she watched wanted a good meal and drink, they could take the train to San Pedro Sula, a larger town situated more than 30 miles away from the coast to protect it from flooding. The banana and sugar companies' offices were based there. Anyone dissatisfied with the food offerings there could continue another 70 or so miles to Tegucigalpa, the capital.

Short on funds, Hurston could not make such excursions for dining, but she, perhaps not unlike those businessmen, was a seasoned traveler. Hurston had sharpened her research skills as a student in Harlem, Haiti, Jamaica, the Bahamas, and the US South, including Florida. She collected Black folklore in the South for one of the New Deal programs that put money back into the pockets of everyday people. At the time, she was in New York, a city that was now less inviting to her and one of her brothers. Irritated by the crime, which was especially worrisome in Harlem, he was leaving the city.

"That is what your blessed New Deal did for us," Hurston told Katherine Tracy L'Engle, a Broadway actress she also tried to lure to Honduras. Hurston was remembering a

1936 civil disturbance in the city. She decided the police were helpless "because the New Deal–promoted Negro politicians immediately let out a scream that Negroes are being persecuted the minute the Negro thug is arrested. I was there, and know that this is what is happening," she said, adding that "the New Deal gang" said the riot was a result of the "poor Negroes" who were "so hungry and down-trodden."[96]

Hurston was certain that communists had instigated it. They also backed Franklin Roosevelt when he made a second bid for the White House.[97] But telling of her contradictory way, she'd heard Roosevelt's "hollow promises" to create an "arsenal of democracy."[98] She was curious about his intentions for the thousands of Black servicemen residing in what she decided was "'arse and all' of democracy."[99] She knew his policies gave African Americans access to federal resources they had not seen since Reconstruction. Then again, on the subject of segregation, she claimed to have "no viewpoint . . . other than a fierce desire for human justice."[100]

It didn't help that she often refused to overtly protest the historically unjust conditions facing African Americans. When Arna Bontemps, the Black poet who made a name for himself alongside Hurston and Hughes in Harlem, reviewed her 1942 memoir *Dust Tracks on a Road* for the *New York Herald Tribune*, he decided she dealt "very simply with the more serious aspects of Negro life in America—she ignores them."[101] He sneered at her political conservatism after also seeing a story she wrote for the *Saturday Evening Post*. As she often did, she took a "swipe at the leftists" in her article.[102] He likely chuckled when he saw the word "Negro" under her byline.[103] She could be heard, but she was still Black like the rest of them.

Many of her peers already frowned at her use of the Black dialect once seen in slave narratives consumed by the white abolitionists. This how we talk, she seemed to say, at least where I'm from. She would not be hushed even when her country pushed wartime propaganda about its greatness. In such an environment, most were mindful of criticizing the nation and especially the government. Aware of the judgment she faced on many fronts, Hurston told W. E. B. Du Bois that white publishers in particular were increasingly afraid and were clamping down on just about anything she had to say.[104] By 1950, she was still so angry, she wrote an essay titled "What White Publishers Won't Print" for *Negro Digest*, a Chicago-based magazine.[105]

None of them could deny her talents. Bontemps wondered whether he should include her work in a children's book about careers. "Lord knows she's a career gal!" he quipped to Hughes.[106] She was ambitious. Writing books had never been enough. She had once been just as excited about Black theater.[107] She'd seen Paul Robeson, Ethel Waters, and Bill "Bojangles" Robinson frequently cast in plays by white writers.[108] "I am now writing music and if I do say so, I have one or two snappy airs," she told Hughes in 1929.[109] "Love old thing. Zora," Hurston closed this letter.[110]

At the time, she was 38 years old. The sign-off was typical of her self-deprecating humor. She was more sensitive about her age than she let on, often taking ten years off when it suited. With Hughes, she could be particularly vulnerable. One letter that she sent him ended with this question: "Do you need some money?"[111] They had been so close, she once told him his letters soothed her "soul like a dreamless sleep."[112] Whatever he and others felt by the 1940s, nothing could undermine how close the two friends had been, and none of their ire could undercut the value of the rich body of writings that she produced in the 1930s, her most productive years. They were also some of the country's most devastating ones.

When Herbert Hoover entered the White House in 1929, there were signs of a pending economic disaster everywhere, but few people could read them. Farmers had too many crops. The top 1 percent of income recipients enjoyed a 75 percent increase in spending money.[113] After he was thrashed in the

1932 election, as David Roediger tells us, Hoover, a Republican who brought industry, labor, and consumer groups together, took a seat on the right as the center shifted left.[114] Although Hurston, a Republican herself, would die penniless and in relative obscurity (that's how bad things would get), by 1975 Alice Walker was singing her praises in *Ms.* magazine, creating the conditions for renewed interest in one of the country's most influential African American female writers, no matter her politics.

New and old fans learned of her collecting folklore from people of African descent and that she was an anthropologist who also critiqued the books of her peers, including Katherine Dunham, the acclaimed Black choreographer-anthropologist. Because Hurston made her research accessible to multiple audiences, she was better known as a writer than as a scholar. *Jonah's Gourd Vine*, her first novel, was published in 1934.[115] The book was inspired by her days in Eatonville, specifically her parents' strained marriage. Within three years, *Their Eyes Were Watching God*, the most celebrated of the seven books she'd see published before her death, was released. For years, the books suggested she was a woman who was never rich but one who was financially stable on occasion. To be sure, things seemed secure for her for a while.

CHAPTER TWO

FINDING A SHIP IN DAYTONA

"It's Almost Ceremonial"

Hurston was in Daytona Beach when she decided to head to Central America. She had bought a houseboat using prize money she'd won for writing *Dust Tracks on a Road*, the 1942 book loosely based on her own life.[1] One Hollywood movie studio analyst learned about how she had grown up in a town "run wholly by and for Negroes."[2] In Eatonville, Florida, this very town, she'd "beat the stuffing out" of her stepmother before working as a maid for a singer and then slowly obtaining an education while making her way to Harlem.[3] The consultant decided that Black people, at least the way she rendered them, were so complicated, "it would require a thesis to disentangle" it all.[4] Hurston seemed to even have contempt for many of her people, he thought.[5] Bontemps was not alone in this critique.[6]

Bontemps sneered at how it came to be that Hurston own a houseboat. He heard about her award and decided that she was able to buy it because of her political views (white moderates and conservatives alike approved of what this Black woman was saying).[7] He did allow that she was more poised than when she first arrived in Harlem.[8] Maybe even more humble. She was definitely still fretting over the fight with fellow Harlem Renaissance writer Langston Hughes, which occurred shortly before she went to Honduras that first time.

To be clear, most folks listening to Hurston talking about Honduras in the mid-1940s may not have known about her three-month research trip there in 1930. She made this voyage around the time she was pursuing fieldwork in the Bahamas. Boas, the esteemed anthropologist, was still directing her work at the very same moment her creative pursuits were getting in the way of her research. Hurston had only recently worked with Hughes on *Mule Bone: A Comedy of Negro Life*, a play. Hughes wanted a third person to share ownership of the work, given her assistance with typing it. Because the book received inspiration from her life, Hurston balked at such an idea and filed a copyright application in her name only. With her ties to Hughes frayed, she headed to Central America. There she wrote Ruth Benedict, one of her professors at Columbia University when Hurston was still trying to pursue a doctoral degree following her studies at Barnard.

That excursion to Honduras was probably an impulsive move and little more than a reconnaissance mission. Hurston was surely aware of how many researchers were heading there during the first half of the twentieth century as US businessmen and government officials were developing relations in that region. She mentioned the various Indigenous groups that could be the subject of fruitful research for "Dr." Benedict, who was hearing from someone who was quite interested in learning the tools of an anthropologist, but also someone who seemed to have had no desire to spend several years in the field studying one subject. Nothing in Honduras at that time had been an urgent enough topic for Hurston to stop working on the other projects before. In the coming years, she juggled manuscripts for folkloric work and novels that received inspiration from her fieldwork elsewhere. Along the way, she never quite got over what she'd done to Hughes. Bontemps noted her concern about that now-gone friendship via letter.

Bontemps had apparently seen her in North Carolina, where she was at the time teaching at a historically Black college in Durham. He assured her that Hughes, her old buddy, "never ceased" to think she was "wonderful."[9] He may have said this because Hurston told him she could get him a job "in the South someplace." On the chance she meant it, Bontemps now wondered whether Hughes would be open to sending "her a sweet letter, or at least send a nice Christmas card."[10] Besides, as he now decided, neither he nor Hughes should "blame poor Zora" for being jealous of the woman who was hired to type *Mule Bone*, the play on which Hughes and Hurston had collaborated. "She can't help it if she's a woman," Bontemps said.[11]

The sexism of her male peers aside, Hurston herself had never been one to hold off on gossiping. Around the time she bought the houseboat, in the spring of 1943, she had a meeting on some unnamed matter with Mary McLeod Bethune, the eminent educator.[12] During the Great Depression, Hurston briefly worked at Bethune-Cookman University, a historically Black institution that Bethune founded. Hurston recalled the difficulties she had getting a light bulb for her office back then.[13] Now, she was back and, as she told one confidante, had heard that a dean at the college was recently and strangely ousted. Bethune and the school's president were rumored to have fled, dodging any responsibility for the act.[14]

If Hurston was at Bethune-Cookman looking for a job, she did not get it. Instead, she settled down in Florida, a state with which she was quite familiar. While collecting folklore there in the 1930s, she climbed into Sassy Susie, her Chevy, wearing a holster, sometimes driving alone. After picking up a recording machine in Jacksonville while working for the WPA, she'd go looking for Black folk to interview. John Lomax, a Library of Congress employee, and Stetson Kennedy, a white writer, would come in next, ready to help.

All of that was behind her. She was on a houseboat that she named *Wanago* ("want to go").[15] She had tried to tempt fate. She would try to sit for a while. Between May 1943 and October 1944, her boat was often moored at a Daytona Beach marina on the Halifax River, which split the town. Rice, sugarcane, cotton, and citrus once grew in the area. By the late nineteenth century, a railroad arrived, jump-starting the economy on a peninsula where most of the money had until now been made upstate. The Seminoles and refugees from slavery had irked the US military that much.

By 1902, Daytona Beach's smooth, white sand attracted race car drivers. Within twelve years, the Panama Canal would widen the prospects of people and products moving on this side of the country. Even as Jim Crow laws hampered Black progress, Roosevelt made James Weldon Johnson a US consul to Venezuela and Nicaragua.[16] Norma Boyd, an African American educator and United Nations observer, represented the States at a conference in Brazil.[17] Hurston had been to the Caribbean several times, but she was now hunkered down and proud to have a boat that was bought and paid for. Even if it needed a little paint and carpentry, it was livable.

"I own a houseboat, the WANAGO," she told Claude Barnett, a Sanford, Florida, native and founder of the Associated Negro Press wire service.[18] The vessel was nearly 20 years old but solidly built. She bragged about her motor, sleeping bunks, and galley. Hurston was clearly excited but also lonely. She invited many to visit.

"I am having an amphibious existence," she told Harold Jackman, a teacher and patron who was also part of her circle in Harlem. "Now don't get any picture in your mind of the Astor yacht. Nothing like that."[19] The cruiser allowed two people to live together comfortably. There was even a toilet "that you can squeeze into and close the door if your behind does not stick out too far," she said.[20] Marjorie Rawlings, the white novelist, learned about the boat's 44-horsepower Gray motor: "How I wish that we could explore both the Indian and St. John's River together."[21]

Few heard about Hurston's marriage in 1944 to James Pitts, a "strong, big wrassly" Cleveland man with a "magnificent brass voice" (who would be really wonderful if only "he had some money," she told Belo).[22] The small quarters probably tested his patience. The boat was too small for her books and papers.[23]

Pitts was the last of her three husbands.[24] While in Jacksonville in 1927, she married Herbert Sheen, a jazz musician and teacher-turned–medical student she met at Howard. Following their divorce a year later, her ex-husband blamed the failed relationship on her career. She went on to have an affair with a singer in a play that she wrote before marrying Albert Price, a man from money several years her junior. She left him too. Now Pitts was gone.

Being there on the Halifax River placed her in a larger story of African Americans thriving in coastal communities. Before the Civil War, Black dockworkers and sailors enjoyed relative freedom from white oversight. In tidal creeks and backwater streams, unsupervised men of African descent, enslaved and free, operated boats and caught fish.[25] Frederick Douglass, who grew up enslaved on Chesapeake Bay, often looked out onto the sea and compared his own condition with the autonomy some had to come and go. One day, he put on a red shirt, a hat, and carelessly tied a black cloth around his neck.[26] Next, he borrowed a certificate carried by merchant mariners.[27] Douglass then fled by train to free territory in Philadelphia.

His courage was seen in others. Robert Smalls, another enslaved African American, was working as a captain for a naval vessel when he escaped from slavery in May 1862 with several crew members.[28] His feat proved valuable to the Union because he took with him a codebook containing Confederate signals as well as maps of the mines and torpedoes in Charleston's harbor. Lincoln recruited Black soldiers to the Union army because of Smalls's efforts.[29]

Women also did the unexpected on or near the sea. Some slipped into men's clothing and worked undetected as sailors for months, even years. Some accompanied husbands who were captains of merchant vessels.[30] A few emerged as heroines outright fighting in wars, looking after lighthouses, and rescuing the shipwrecked on both sides of the Atlantic.[31]

If she was not conscious of making a statement, Hurston was part of a small population who lived afloat by the mid-twentieth century. She likely learned quite a bit about the rigors of the mariner's life while conducting fieldwork. One of her bosses from the days when she was gathering material on the "Florida Negro" during the Depression recounted Hurston's familiarity with boats and waterways when speculating about the *Clotilda*.[32] The sunken ship was believed to have carried the last shipment of enslaved people from Africa to Alabama shortly before the Civil War began. Hurston wanted to see it raised from the bottom of the Alabama river and towed to Jacksonville.[33]

She likely learned about the boat after her 1927 interview with Cudjoe Lewis, a captured man who traveled on it from Dahomey.[34] Unconcerned about the impracticality of her idea given its then-limited audience in the South, she maintained that if recovered, the *Clotilda* should be restored and tour the state of Florida by water. She guessed that it was in "very shallow water just above Mobile," and although "it would be a long tow" the boat could be "exhibited all the way down the gulf from Mobile to Fort Meyers, cross the state through Lake Okeechobee, and into the Indian River at Stuart, then up the river to Jacksonville, taking several months, and exhibited" from town to town.[35]

Living on a river may have inspired Hurston's proposition. She was likely the only, or one of a few, African Americans at the marina where the *Wanago* was moored. As she told Rawlings, all the other boat owners were very nice to her. "Not a word about race," she added.[36] Elizabeth Howard, the daughter of the man who owned the marina, recalled sitting at a little table in the *Wanago* with Hurston. Wearing a brown turban,

Hurston told stories, including one about "how black people got black."[37] "I loved Zora's stories, and I loved Zora," Howard recalled.[38]

Hurston had long charmed the whites around her. Hughes remembered how during her early years in Harlem, white patrons "simply paid her just to sit around and represent the Negro race for them."[39] She "could make you laugh one minute and cry the next."[40] But she was strategic in orchestrating gaiety. She often wanted something from the ones laughing, and they themselves sometimes wanted something beyond entertainment from her, too. When Rawlings told Hurston that she needed help with housekeeping, Hurston obliged her, sleeping outside in the maid's quarters. She even fawned over one of Rawlings's books that said a raccoon's paws looked like a "nigger baby's hands."[41] Rawlings had, after all, helped her get signed on with Scribner's after Lippincott, her initial publisher, began rejecting Hurston's manuscripts.[42] Besides, working for white people provided another opportunity to write and sell another story. Shortly after that visit, Hurston wrote an essay about how whites needed a "pet Negro" who seemed exceptional when compared to other African Americans,[43] who had their "pet whites," too, Hurston decided.[44]

Her wit likely positioned her to get other white boat owners on the Halifax to show her how to manage her boat's plumbing, electrical, and mechanical systems. When she left the marina, she would have also needed to learn to manage changes in the wind, tides, and bridge clearances. Depending on how far she got, Hurston would have also needed to know the location of docks and mooring spots where she could anchor for free or for a modest fee.

She was surely thoughtful when she entered the shops where white boaters stocked up on provisions in the segregated South. Hurston might have been privy to information about the places where a low tide might expose oysters, providing food, or land where fruit could be picked from trees. If she piloted the boat 1,500 miles to New York, as some have suggested, she would have to know how to anchor her boat on the Hudson River.[45]

To also ensure her safety, she had to know that some communities were more hostile to liveaboards than others. She would have known that the Coast Guard had the right to board and search any vessel without a warrant. Had she been subjected to such a search and attitudes, it would have been in keeping with what other African Americans and women had suffered.

As would be the case in Honduras, until she made some money, she had to be frugal in Florida. But the hull need to be painted. There was also a motor and pump issue. The "darned thing has kept me as broke," she told one confidante.[46] Hurston also needed another pair of hands to help pull on the ropes when she wanted to dock. She told Jackman that she wished that he and Countee Cullen, another poet of her Harlem circle, would come down for a few weeks this summer and "rough it some."[47]

*

She had always managed. The fifth of eight children, she routinely asked white snowbirds passing through Eatonville if she could walk with them for a while. They were amenable and even mailed books back for her to read. Her grandmother, a former enslaved woman, looked on worriedly. After her mother died, Hurston was shuttled between her siblings and working odd jobs after quarreling with her father's new wife. Along the way, she lived in Jacksonville, Memphis, and Baltimore. In 1918, the same year her father died, she graduated from the night school arm of present-day Morgan State University. Her twenty-sixth birthday was behind her, although most did not know this.

When she arrived at Morgan, she owned a single dress, a pair of underwear, and the shoes on her feet.[48] She moved to Washington, DC, where she attended Howard University. Her conversations with Alain Locke, her professor there, led her to Harlem. By 1925, Hurston was winning prizes for her writing. That same year, she enrolled at Barnard, where she was summoned to teas by her white classmates. She was, however, discouraged when her classmates said they would exchange dances with the date accompanying her to a prom held at the Ritz-Carlton if he were "as light" as herself.[49] Seeing their limited thinking, though not fretting too much over it, Hurston did not attend the gathering. She explained away her absence by saying she did not have enough money to buy a new dress.

Her money woes were finally solved when she began working for Hurst, the white novelist for whom she'd made that holiday card foretelling her days in Honduras. Hurst discovered that Hurston was a better writer than a secretary. She introduced her to Charlotte Osgood Mason, a white Manhattan socialite who funded other artists and writers, including Hughes. A charmer even then, Hurston called Mason "Godmother." With $200 a month—$3,000 in today's currency—a camera, and a car, she began to gather folktales.[50] But Mason, who funded much of Hurston's research beginning in 1927, wanted to know every penny she spent. She even mentioned the 65 cents she spent on sanitary napkins in one letter.[51] Mason not only funded Hurston's research; she legally owned it, creating tensions that might have been anticipated. The two women parted ways in 1932, not long after Hurston gave up on completing her doctoral studies at Columbia, and not long after she visited Honduras the first time.

This second trip to the country was set in motion following a visit by Reginald Brett, an English miner, and his wife aboard the *Wanago* in the summer of 1944. The Bretts had traveled to Honduras, where they mined gold and claimed to have become familiar with the ruins of a lost Mayan city "that no other white person" had seen.[52] He claimed they contained a buried treasure. Having read Hurston's *Tell My Horse: Voodoo and Life in Haiti and Jamaica*, her 1938 book that featured the folkloric work she had collected in Haiti and Jamaica, Brett suggested Hurston find the ruins.[53]

The friends who were reluctant to travel with her were probably skeptical of such a daunting and costly expedition. Even the Guggenheim Foundation, which had twice funded her research in the West Indies, had doubts. She told Henry Allen Moe, who administered funds for the organization, some of the things she earlier told Benedict in 1930: there were several Indigenous groups and medicinal plants worth studying.[54] Again, her first visit to Honduras occurred the year after she'd done field work in the Bahamas.

Hurston offered few details about the ruin, merely that there was an undisturbed cemetery of the "Ancient Mayans" on Honduras's northeastern coast.[55] Moe asked her to write a proposal that might justify his group paying her expenses.[56] She barely revised what she earlier shared but did add that she wanted to study "Old Spanish" music, too. She likely thought such music should be included because growing foreign investment in Central America had led to increased cultural interest in this part of the world, too.

Many people wanted the sounds of the tropics in their living rooms. Afro-Brazilian and other music from south of the border was booming on the soundtracks of early to mid-twentieth-century movies and, later, television shows as well as vinyl records.[57] The anthropologist in her was evidently interested in the roots of some of these beautiful sounds. Her efforts were to no avail. The Guggenheim passed on giving Hurston the generous two-year research grant.[58]

By now, her friend Belo had heard about Fred Irvine, a 31-year-old Englishman who owned the *Maridome*, a 27-ton schooner.[59] He promised to take her down.[60] Irvine cared little about anthropology, and it was just as well. Hurston needed his skills on the sea. He agreed to allow her to charter his ship for "unlimited research in the tropics."[61] In exchange for hitching a ride, she would get the ship repainted and stock it with provisions and new sails. In other words, she would have to " 'find' the ship," as she said, showing off her recently acquired knowledge.[62]

In another letter that Hurston sent to Belo and her husband, Frank Tannenbaum, a scholar who had also attended Columbia and conducted research in Mexico, Hurston said that the *Maridome* needed some canvas to create a "nice sitting spot. That will be important in the tropics, you know."[63] To cut down on expenses, she and Irvine were taking the schooner down the Indian River about 200 miles to a repair facility near West Palm Beach and decided to do the paint job themselves. "I have learned to do a good job of boat-painting in these two years of ownership," said Hurston. "I can use a blow-torch with the best. . . . It is almost ceremonial."[64]

The money that she was spending must have raised eyebrows. Irvine had inherited a bit of money—or so Hurston said. But she was footing the bill to repair his ship as well as paying for its upkeep and other provisions during the voyage and long stay in Central America.[65] Even if he was giving her a lift to Honduras, her friends doubtless had many questions about whether this was a fair exchange, particularly because she was also asking them for their unpaid research assistance and boat repair labor.

Hurston predicted the preparations would take no more than six weeks. The mahogany walls in the boat's salon were warped and cracked. She would have to pay the carpenter to replace it.[66] To the list of things she needed were a tropical wool skirt for herself and tropical pants for Irvine for when they went ashore in Havana and elsewhere. "He must have the fancy pants," she said.[67] Going without them and "some beautiful Senorita" would be awful for him. The repairs and supplies would cost $800, an amount she could handle. "I already have commitments with publishers for stuff after I get there, so I know that I shall not starve," she said.

There was more on Hurston's mind, though. Irvine seemed to want to bring along a female companion, and Hurston didn't think this was wise, as the woman had strong political opinions that might hurt Hurston's research efforts. Irvine's friend was "a damned imperialist and would flap her big mouth and turn the Indians and perhaps all the Hondurians [*sic*] against us," Hurston decided.[68] They should all be careful because, as Hurston put it, "Latin America is not fond of Americans," because of the tensions spilling over from the States' historic surveillance of this part of the world even as Franklin Roosevelt tried to take a more hands-off approach. Still, "months of careful behavior" were in order, Hurston decided.[69] She knew the wrong person along could result in months of work being "torn down."[70]

While trying to persuade others to travel with her, a category 4 hurricane hit Cuba, and 300 people were killed. The storm made landfall in Sarasota, heading across the peninsula to Florida's east coast. Hurston, who survived a 1929 hurricane in the Bahamas, was barely unnerved by the rough surf and torrential rainfall. As the rain poured, she wrote Belo and her husband that if the three of them reached the ruin first, they would have "the world by the ears."[71] As if the hurricane was serious but incidental to her life, she added, "This boat is rearing and pitching like a mule in a tin stable. But I am not distressed. The boat is sound. I like the violent aspects of nature, (if I am safe)."[72] Her words demonstrate how she valued her physical safety even if she sometimes dangerously flirted with death.

The bad weather must have at last made it impossible to write. She scribbled "Tropical hurricane is raging" at the top of one page of a letter to the Guggenheim.[73] The *Wanago* must have suffered some damage during the storm. By April 1945 she was receiving mail at a dwelling at 644 South Seagrave Street in Daytona Beach.[74] Within two months, she was residing on another houseboat, this one named the *Sun Tan*.[75] Whether she owned it is unclear. The storm must have given her a moment to assess her own mortality because she reached out to Du Bois, whom she addressed as the "Dean of American Negro Artists," with another grand proposal.[76] She told him that he should see about securing 100 acres in Florida for a cemetery holding the bodies of the "illustrious Negro dead."[77] They would include Frederick Douglass and Nat Turner, leader of a failed 1831 slave revolt. The latter's "bones have long since gone to dust," she wrote, "but that should not prevent his tomb being among us." She added, "Let no Negro celebrity, no matter what financial condition they might be in death, lie in inconspicuous forgetfulness."[78] Perhaps she was already wondering about how her own legacy would be shaped. Finding the Mayan ruin would ensure she would not be forgotten.

*

If all else failed, while down in Honduras, she could take pleasure in being seen as a US citizen and all that this entailed. Al Jennings, a confidante of O. Henry, embraced his citizenship when he visited Honduras in the early twentieth century.[79] He recounted, in an evidently tall tale, attending a Fourth of July celebration at the governor's mansion in Trujillo, another port town on the Honduran north coast. There, "a negro" was "brought along for the sake of democracy."[80] Just as the Americans stood to sing "The Star-Spangled Banner," they were interrupted by an uprising. "Gentlemen, the natives are trying to steal our copyrighted Fourth," someone said.[81] Jennings and his comrades reportedly became heroes only because the Royal Army began gaining on the rebels when the Americans also scurried. A "little maid" tried to join them as they darted to a boat; for years, he and his friends would remember the "strip of brown muslin" they left behind.[82] Music expanded the possibilities of stories told via books. Indeed, this little maid was the direct opposite of the "tall and tan, young and lovely" girl in a beachside Brazilian town.[83] This is the one from Ipanema about whom many have sung, the one who likely chuckles as "each one she passes goes, 'Ah.'"[84]

*

Hurston, too, looked straight ahead toward the approximate location of the ruin she hoped to find on the northeast coast of Honduras. She discovered that Doris Zemurray Stone, a white US archaeologist, had also traveled to the northeast coast, looking for the same Mayan city. Hurston took delight in discovering how Stone's guides "messed her up" so much, she did not get far. The locals apparently persuaded her "there was nothing to see," as Hurston told her editor.[85] In her view, these Indigenous guides were just outsmarting another American, who, as it shall be shown, descended from someone making money on, above all, the banana, a fruit traced to Malaysia although its name comes from Cameroon.[86]

During the late nineteenth century, Minor Cooper Keith, the son of a Brooklyn lumber merchant, experimented with the fruit.[87] He first went to Central America to build a rail line in Costa Rica. In fact, in 1883, he married into a prominent Costa Rican family, which positioned him favorably.[88] But it was on the banana that he would make his fortune. With his three brothers beside him for a time, and the sweat of an ample workforce made up of, first, Black West Indians and, next, immigrants from northern Italy, he finally completed construction on the line and established his banana plantations. He made so much on the latter, he sent his surplus stock to New Orleans.

The US government was wary of monopolies and watched him closely. Keith decided to merge his fruit business with that of Andrew Preston, of Boston. They created the United Fruit Company, which would go on to corner the market on fruit in Central America under Samuel Zemurray, or "Sam the Banana Man."[89] Zemurray had seen the government's surveillance and transportation headaches, even as the tourists, businessmen, and the sex workers arrived.[90] After learning Spanish and cajoling the local growers, he was poised to achieve phenomenal success. Not unlike Keith, he secured land and tax concessions from Central American countries, too.

Zemurray, notably, was not American. He immigrated to the States from Russia when he was 14 years old. He saw a banana for the first time while he was living in Selma, Alabama, 94 miles east of Notasulga, where Hurston was born.[91] The enterprising Zemurray went south to Mobile and New Orleans, learning various trades. The latter city alongside New York played a huge role in the rise of the banana trade that would eventually interest him.[92] By 1901, he had bought forests using $200,000 from investors in New Orleans, Mobile, and New York.[93] He continued to see the trust busters as well as United Fruit's ongoing cash flow issues. By 1929, he sold stock in his company to United Fruit and took a huge stake in that company, which he oversaw until he retired in 1951.

His wealth was tied to his ability to grow fruit but also to build the bridges and railroads that moved his produce to the marketplace. And beyond dominating the produce market in the Caribbean, United Fruit also funded research missions such as the reconnaissance visit to Honduras made by researchers from Tulane University and the Danish National Museum, which the two groups recounted in their 1938 report.[94] However, these scholars and others heading south to Central America benefited from the discoveries of the engineers, foremen, workers, and overseers who, while excavating for the United Fruit Company's roads, railroads, and bridges, were often the first to uncover the Indigenous objects that were later considered artifacts.[95]

Stone, the archaeologist that Hurston ridiculed, benefited from her ties to the company: Zemurray was her father. On the one hand, this advantage undermined her reputation as a serious researcher; Hurston believed Stone approached archaeology in an "ameteurish [sic]" way. On the other hand, the heiress likely inspired professional jealousy tied to Stone having the doctoral degree that Hurston gave up on earning. "Don't bother about me. You could never understand me. Cordially yours, Dr. Zora Neale Hurston Lit. D."[96] These words survive as a fragment on a piece of paper. The date she wrote these words is unclear. The person who first read them is unclear, too. Perhaps that individual knew she'd stopped her doctoral training. The reader may have known she was referring to an honorary degree that Morgan State had given her. She would never have an endowed teaching chair or oversee a major institution like Stone at the National Museum of Costa Rica. Nor did Hurston have a husband with the funds to invest in a coffee plantation.[97] And while Hurston's father owned land in Eatonville, Stone grew up in a mansion across the street from Tulane, where many of the artifacts of several expeditions in Honduras were stored.[98] Academic, political, and business interests were clearly aligned in a modernizing world where success, particularly the financial kind, was the end goal. Hurston had navigated this economy from a small all-Black town in Florida to become part of an empire that included Henry Ford, the father of mass production. Stone's father was the first to do the same down in Honduras. The "Big Mike," a banana with a thick skin that resulted in less bruising during shipment, was the favored pick over the more than 300 varieties.⁹⁹ The heat and moisture in Honduran low-land on the north coast was perfect for it; although cultivated in Iceland and Israel, the banana thrived best in rainy, tropical places with great drainage.¹⁰⁰

Hurston would have seen banana plants growing between 6 and nearly 30 feet. Given her ongoing intestinal problems, she probably knew the fruit helps with everything from stomach-ache to constipation. It even helps regulate one's blood sugar and has mood-lifting properties similar to those of ecstasy and Prozac. Rubbing the inside of its skin on a mosquito bite can ease itching.

Zemurray stood to gain much from the product, as the banana and Central America made their way into popular culture in the years ahead. Two postwar films demonstrate as much. A weeping white Manhattan bride (Barbara Garrick) in the 1988 motion picture *Working Girl* worried about her whether her elaborate, floor-length wedding dress might be mistaken for a political statement on Nicaragua. Agador Spartacus, the dancing gay maid (Hank Azaria) in the 1997 movie *The Birdcage*, thought his boss was threatened by his "Guatelmalan-ness," his "natural heat."¹⁰¹ Even in the 2017 comedy *Girls Trip*, an African American woman (Jada Pinkett Smith) is teased for wanting to wear a Guatemalan-styled dress out to party with her girlfriends in New Orleans.¹⁰² Laughter had by now been heard for years. During the 1930s and 1940s, the Portuguese singer Carmen Miranda sang and danced in the movies, wearing a hat decorated with fruit, including the banana. At virtually the same time, people began using the term "going bananas" to refer to insanity. By midcentury, Harry Belafonte's "Banana Boat Song" captured the joy of Caribbean stevedores singing "Daay-oo" as their night shift ended.

Given its phallic shape, the banana was ideal for dirty postcards. United Fruit's own marketing team declared any banana under nine inches substandard. Amid such marketing efforts, racial anxieties grew, especially after the *Windrush*, a boat once used by the Germans, took Black West Indians to England in 1948 to fill a labor shortage. White Englishman feared these migrants would take their jobs and women.[103] The extent of the xenophobia was revealed in a race riot in the Notting Hill district of London.

West Indians could be reluctant to recall their long-standing suffering on both sides of the pond. Hazel Carby, a scholar and daughter of a white Welsh woman and a Jamaican man, recalled her father's aversion to speaking about the "difficult times" in Jamaica, until Black protestors in England in the 1960s reminded him of exploited Black workers demonstrating in his homeland in the late 1930s.[104] Suddenly, the former Royal Air Force airman made the connection between two islands. He was ready to talk, saying "how terrible, how very, very terrible it was."[105] Carby was finally no longer in Yorkshire, protesting on the streets of Kingston in 1938 after the cane fields were burned. She pondered the impact of people sailing toward and away from each other, as writers had before her.[106]

In her 1936 novel *Voyage in the Dark,* Jean Rhys followed a West Indian girl who arrives in London where thousands of white people rush past dark houses that seem to frown. They were running and she was running, too, not unlike Hurston and the others crossing borders, including the ones who get to Mexico only to hear, "Go back. Wait." This West Indian girl represented those who, as Tina Campt has told us, dreamed of a "future beyond Empire," until crushed, "smack in the heart of the metropole."[107] White eyes linger upon them because their oppressed bodies have been overlooked for so long, they still seem new.[108] Sam Selvon's 1956 *The Lonely Londoners* presents West Indians who, in an attempt to fight racism, possibly knew that it was best to "stay in the world you belong to and you don't know about what happening in the other ones except what you read in the papers."[109] An elderly West

Indian woman explained it this way: "I tell all of them who coming, 'why all you leaving the country to go to England? Over there is so cold that only white people does live there.' But they say that it have more work in England, and better pay."[110] The banana, a symbol of Western prosperity, helped put money in people's pockets, some more than others.

Stone's father had contributed to this development. He had been crafty. Unhappy upon hearing the news that he would receive no break on products coming through the customs house, he engineered a coup against Honduran president Miguel Dávila. The ordeal inspired *Appointment in Honduras*, a 1953 film about a white man from the States who must get money to a president facing a coup in a fictitious Central American country. He confronts adversaries who include a wealthy "American" and his double-crossing wife, who is dressed in a nightgown—of all things—for most of the movie. He must also contend with the Spanish-speaking prisoners who want his money belt, Honduran soldiers pursuing them all, and the menace of reptiles, animals, and insects, none of which stopped the Yankee from delivering his money to the Central American president.[111]

A more humorous white savior is seen in a 1971 Woody Allen film aptly titled *Bananas*.[112] Allen plays Fielding Mellish, a working-class *gringo* from New York who wants to impress his social activist girlfriend. He travels to San Marcos, yet another fictitious banana republic. The viewer sees more rebels and running soldiers. Predictably, the Yankee unintentionally becomes radical and the most suitable person to be the president of a Central American country.

Gabriel García Márquez's 1967 novel *One Hundred Years of Solitude* revealed the hazards of the infighting in Central America with his beloved Colombia in view. The massacre of hundreds of Central American workers occurred in 1928, a year before he was born.[113] So many of these published writings, songs, and motion pictures tell a similar story of a conquered land and people, where some of the most deprived turn on each other.

The work practices in Honduras were little better than during the era of slavery when white overseers, some of the lowliest in the Southern social hierarchy, abused the enslaved.[114] Many of the men overseeing Black workers in Honduras during the early twentieth century were from the US South. Clashes were frequent. In 1910, a Jamaican man was lynched, but United Fruit still hired the *ladino* man who committed the atrocity, and he faced no serious consequences.[115] As Lara Putnam has written in her study of the interwar efforts of British Caribbean workers to secure employment abroad, hostile attitudes toward immigrants were pervasive in Honduras, Cuba, Costa Rica, and British Caribbean locales. They could expect "abuse, malignity and violence," which increased as the young century matured and fortunes were made.[116] Within three years, as much as $18 million worth of bananas were imported into the United States.[117] United became so influential, its ships were used by the States during the failed 1961 Bay of Pigs invasion in Cuba.[118] The company had earlier demonstrated that it could switch out a government if it wanted with Dávila's fall. United would eventually collapse in part because of the financial losses it suffered by the 1970s and in part as an outcome of lawsuits over the harmful effects of its pesticides on banana workers.

Elvia Alvarado, a Honduran human rights activist, saw the horrors firsthand. She was hesitant but decided the world should know more about people like her, *campesinos*, or peasants, in Central America, who lived in houses made of bamboo, sugar cane, or corn stalks.[119] Her father was one. He scrounged up money by working various day jobs.[120] Her mother supplemented her husband's income by baking bread and raising chickens and pigs. But her parents split because her father was abusive. One of seven children, Alvarado had to figure out how to raise herself. Perhaps the three señoras that Hurston heard moaning had to do the same themselves and turned to one of the oldest options available to them. These women, like others, were running from something huge and sometimes dangerous, too: dependency on men, families, and governments that needed them but were not able or inclined to see to their best interests.

In a book published in 1987, a time when the United States was still preoccupied with instability in Central America amid ongoing fears of communism, Alvarado relayed the woes of the women workers trying to organize as their husbands opposed their growing militancy.[121] Meanwhile, the army recruited poor boys with few options, and rebels hid in the forests, as the *gringos*, who did not even know why they were in Central America, routinely sexually abused women and girls.[122] Alvarado wondered how anyone could stand by and not do anything.

"Maybe it sounds like I have my head in the clouds," she wrote, adding, "But I've heard about these astronauts in the United States who've gone into outer space. And I figure, hell, if these astronauts can get to the moon, then why can't ordinary folks like us learn to share the earth?"[123] Statistics bear out her words. In 1979, as much 56 percent of the wealth in Honduras went to just 20 percent of the population. By 1984, rural Honduran workers could expect little more than $25 per month. The disparities persisted even though the government and United Fruit conceded to some worker demands after a 1954 strike: although a *campesino* could own land that United Fruit owned but was not using by 1975, getting the land was difficult.[124] Redistributing the unused property would take as long as 103 years.

The poor had spoken their piece. Some died doing so: in 1975, the Honduran military led a massacre against its own people. Meanwhile, the States used the country as a base to fight radicals, especially in Nicaragua and El Salvador. The Americans built airstrips, a command and logistics center, and other things. But the CIA-trained "contras," right-wing counterrevolutionary fighters, needed guns. To get them, the States secretly sold arms to Iran, making headlines when the sales were exposed. Alvarado continued to live in the second-poorest nation in the Western Hemisphere, behind only Haiti.[125] She saw people disappear. Some were illegally detained and even assassinated. When Hurston turned her head away from local politics, she veered away from these matters, but not entirely. She was, after all, trying to recover a bit of Mayan history. Indigenous people who lived hundreds and even thousands of years ago had also suffered. She'd redeem herself on this front.

CHAPTER THREE

SEEING "DIFFUSED PINKNESS"

What More Could She Want?

Before she headed for the Mayan ruin, Hurston needed to first write a draft of *Seraph on the Suwanee*, her seventh book and the last to be published in her lifetime. Unlike her earlier writings, *Seraph* departed from her usual focus on Black folk. Her lead character was a turn-of-the-century white woman who admits to being little more than "trash," and who, sadly, leaves her happiness in the hands of an abusive husband.[1] At the time Hurston was writing this book, she was seeking success in Hollywood.

She had seen the possibilities when she was out on the West Coast in 1941. A white dancer was concerned about Hurston's bout with malaria. She had studied rituals in Bali, where she also ran a clinic, and her mother had tried to enhance the lives of women in California. She suggested going to Los Angeles for medical attention and to rest up.

Hurston and the dancer were soon touring the Sierra Nevada range, which Hurston found was not anything like resting up at all. Even if she'd once scribbled some mountains on a greeting card, Hurston grew up in flat Florida. She believed that "land is supposed to lie down and be walked on—not rearing up, staring you in the face."[2] Besides, a person has "just so many places to bump" down a rocky cliff.

While out there, Hurston reluctantly wrote her memoir. She also made some extra cash by working as a script consultant for Paramount. She stayed as long as she could bear being surrounded by leftists.

Key Zora Neale Hurston Movements - 1940s

Rhinebeck
New York
Los Angeles
Chapel Hill Durham
Beaufort Atlantic
Mobile Ocean
St. Augustine
Daytona Beach
Gulf of
Mexico
Miami
Beach
Miami Nassau

Legend
→ Travels in Honduras
○ Locations Visited

Pacific
Ocean

Puerto Cortes
Ceiba Mosquito Coast
Santa Rosa de
Copán Tegucigalpa

Caribbean
Sea

0   250   500   750   1,000 mi   University of Alabama Cartographic Research Lab
alabamamaps.ua.edu

Made with data
from the USGS

Zora Neale Hurston's travels in the 1940s.
Courtesy of the University of Alabama Cartographic Lab.

In the early 1940s, a "new belligerence" emerged among African Americans in Los Angeles. Although he lived in Harlem, labor organizer A. Philip Randolph was a well-known face in LA for his leadership of the sleeping porters union. In June 1941, he successfully demanded that Roosevelt ban discrimination in the defense industry. Local Black activists promised the LAPD Vice Squad that they would "meet force with force" if the harsh treatment of people of African descent in the defense industries on the West Coast and elsewhere continued.[3]

Meanwhile, local Black Angelenos were also angered over the KKK resurfacing in the area. In 1940, African American beachgoers were attacked while relaxing on Santa Monica Beach. The same year, 15 Black mess attendants stationed on the USS *Philadelphia* were arrested after publicly expressing their unhappiness over demeaning work assignments via a letter to the *Pittsburgh Courier*, the most influential Black newspaper in the country.[4] Two were jailed. There was anger in this once-sleepy city, founded in 1781 with Black and biracial settlers.[5] Unfortunately, by the interwar period, as the movie industry grew, most businesses outside of segregated communities, including those near Central Avenue, refused Black patrons entry. And yet, in this same area, by the 1940s, Duke Ellington's much-heralded stage show *Jump for Joy* opened at the Mayan Theatre in the heart of downtown.[6] Whereas most down-and-out Black folks were clueless about a renaissance in Harlem, Ellington attracted a mixture of people, white and Black, among them "scuffling-type Negroes."[7] His show was performed 101 times before it closed.

Ellington's stunning achievement recalls the earlier accomplishments of the Indigenous people for whom the theater in which his show premiered was named. But Blacks in his day still faced great suffering not unlike the Mayans themselves had. This was the case particularly as the entertainment industry, as true even now, was anxious to review material about African Americans. What they did with it after seeing it was another matter. Many of the writers who had participated in the Harlem Renaissance were aware of the hurdles in Hollywood. Hurston, Arna Bontemps, Langston Hughes, Jessie Fauset, Richard Wright, Claude McKay, and other African Americans all sent their work out west.[8] They were all part of the so-called "Niggerati," a term that Hurston coined to mock the irony in being, at least in the minds of some, "niggers" producing literary work with lasting merit in bookstores if not on the silver screen.[9]

When she sat down to write *Seraph*, Hurston wanted to make it big in Hollywood so much, she wrote a novel featuring white characters. This tactic was also her way of contesting the rules that said African Americans should never write about white people.[10] Other writers, including Ann Petry and Wallace Thurman, had done the same.[11] So did Hughes, who over the years continued to received updates on Hurston from Bontemps. When Hurston relocated to the West Coast in 1941 to improve her chances of selling her work to a Hollywood producer, Bontemps told Hughes that he heard she was in Pasadena.[12] He shared how she had offended the hosts of a dinner being given in her honor by not showing up.[13] As had been the case in numerous northern cities (and elsewhere in the Americas, including the northern coast of Honduras), Black folks there were wary of newcomers.[14] Perhaps feeling the disdain, Hurston left Pasadena altogether. "Did I tell you Zora is living in Los Angeles proper now?" Hughes later gossiped.[15] Bontemps then bragged it was he who sent her west: "I drew the usual Chamber of Commerce picture of the place."[16]

No matter the sniping, they were all chasing a deal. "Have been having some conferences with movie producers, but no results," Hughes told Bontemps about his own failure. "I think only a subsidized Negro Film Institute, or the revolution will cause any really good Negro picture to be made in America . . . right now."[17] Aware of the war raging against the backdrop of their Tinseltown dreams, he decided the movie industry needed Black writers in order to boost the country's commitment to democracy. He lamented how more people saw a Paramount movie in a single day than read a book written by a "Negro" writer.[18]

Hurston, as was often the case, bypassed all that direct talk about race. If she was going to deal with that subject, she would not spend too much energy whining, at least not in the way so many did. She would unveil the nuances in such conversations. She would think through how Black and white people sometimes shared power, particularly in places where nature could do them all in. One such place was the ocean. That she used it as the setting for *Seraph* is unsurprising. She was writing on a waterfront and had spent time on many waterfronts. Though she had no use for formal labor strikes engineered by reactionary leftists, she could see how the lowliest independently, if not collectively, made demands, however small, on the most powerful. Few sit idly allowing unjust acts to repeatedly affect them without responding.

She prepared to write this particular novel even before she left for Central America. While living in Daytona Beach, she went out on a shrimp boat and observed its operations.[19] Hurston biographer Robert Hemenway has said her use of shrimping in *Seraph* was merely a way to show off what she had learned.[20] As Valerie Boyd, a subsequent Hurston biographer, has acknowledged, the *New York Times* did allow the following: "The author knows her people, the Florida crackers of the swamps and turpentine camps intimately."[21] In *Seraph*, Hurston turned away from those swamps and camps. She looked to the ocean, and the people on it, as scholar John Charles has written.[22] All of them.

Set in a small town on Florida's west coast, *Seraph* first looks at Arvay Meserve, a frightfully insecure young woman who admits to being little more than "white trash."[23] But Jim, who becomes a farmer selling bootleg liquor on the side, courts and quickly marries her. A Portuguese tenant on land that Jim buys farther east helps him learn another skill: shrimping. That a foreigner, and moreover, one from a country south of the US border, is key to a pivotal change in Arvay's life is unsurprising. Neither is the name of Arvay's mother: María. There are lots of Marias in Honduras. Hurston may have overheard more than the señoras' moans. Maybe a repeat customer called one of these women by this name.

Arvay's most urgent goal is to save her marriage. She and Jim have become distant. Two of their three children have left home. The other has tragically died. Arvay will mend her marriage by the sea, where Jim feels most alive. Arvay must make the sea her life, if she is to have a happy marriage.

Arvay is on the run, too. She follows Jim to New Smyrna Beach. By the time she gets there, he owns three shrimping boats, including the *Arvay Henson*.[24] The vessel pays homage to her maiden name. Jim behaves in beastly ways, but he acknowledges the woman he met before she was married to him.

In joining Jim, Arvay seems to lack the strength of Janie Mae, the protagonist in Hurston's *Their Eyes*.[25] Janie left not one but two husbands before taking up with Teacake, a young man who seems fearless even if he is broke—money ain't everything. He loves Janie and whatever he has belongs to her, and they build a life together. He doesn't even need the money she has inherited from her most recent husband. They traipse through the fields near Lake Okeechobee before a hurricane ends their amazing love affair.

Via Arvay and Janie, Hurston sorted through power dynamics between men and women, Blacks and whites, but also human beings more generally. When she updated her editor on her progress, she even felt comfortable enough to tell this man how she'd discovered the limits of relationships. She recalled that one of her beaus sulked at a Harlem party, thinking she had taken him to the shindig only to show him what a "big shot" she was.[26] The fellow in question "had a good mind," but his poor sense of self was surprising.[27] She saw how being competitive could hurt a relationship and mapped out this dynamic in *Seraph*. Indeed, Arvay fears Jim's success as a shrimper: if he becomes too good at anything, he might not need her. Hurston's lover in Harlem apparently felt the same way. Through Arvay, a plain-looking southern white woman, Hurston also sorted through her own losses, including her own beauty, or lack thereof, as she aged: she told her editor that she was no longer worried about her "homely" looks.[28]

Arvay's insecurities irritate her husband. He leaves her for a life on the Atlantic Ocean. After burying her mother, Arvay follows the man who was a devoted provider, even if he once raped her. Arvay was a handful, but she had also tolerated much.

Jim is surprised to see her. He quickly sends home the African American couple who drove her. He is unmindful that they wanted to enjoy a break by the sea, too. Moving forward with his wife is the most important thing.

Jim outfits Arvay in "blue jeans that the fishermen wore ... and the tall rubber sea-boots."[29] The next morning, she learns about the duties of his shrimping crew, which includes an African American man and a third mate whose racial identity is more uncertain, not unlike many of the people passing Hurston in Honduras. The three awaken at five o'clock to warm their engines. The men on nearby boats do the same. After tending to chores, they all head to sea. Arvay is with them.

She almost immediately notices that power there seems to be shared: "there were as many if not more colored captains than white on the dock," and like that marina where Hurston's boat was anchored in Daytona Beach, "nobody thought anything about it. White and Negro captains were friendly together and compared notes. Some boats had mixed crews."[30] This is the South no one wanted to talk about but Hurston.

Readers of *Seraph* do not always know whether the speaker is white or Black because Hurston believed the southern dialect was jointly created. The southerners' vernacular does not belong to the white or the Black speaker but to the southerner.[31] And such speech is the closest to what might be call the "purest English" in the United States.[32] Hurston declared that the old language, customs, songs, ways of speaking, and even beliefs can, indeed, be captured in the southerner, no matter the color of one's skin.[33]

This is to be expected of Hurston, who had routinely studied what separated and brought folks together. She once told Hughes, her old buddy, that Black Bahamians were "more African" than African Americans and "actually know the tribe from which their ancestors come."[34] In making these kinds of comparisons in *Seraph*, she did something else; she blurred borders in the so-called New World. Of late, scholars have increasingly done the same, declaring that the answer to labor shortages in Cuba and Virginia (importing captured Africans) is a reminder of the ties between the US south and the rest of the Americas.[35] Even the way certain countries are cataloged is worth rethinking. Joshua Jelly-Schapiro has suggested that because the Caribbean Sea is bounded by Mexico, Central and South America, and the Antilles, even the Yucatan Peninsula is worthy of being bundled with the Caribbean region.[36] Sometimes people on this side of the Atlantic shape themselves with the land in mind. Indeed, Black Colombians residing on the northern coast of their country, on the Caribbean Sea, are identified as the *costeños*, named on the basis of where they reside.[37] Meanwhile, the Black Caribs, particularly the Garifuna ethnic group, tend to embrace their African heritage even as they live near the same sea.[38] In either case, the sea is an important place for people who descended from the captured African who survived the Middle Passage. Waterways are a place where Black people, as was true of Hurston when she owned a boat in Florida, often have some say in matters concerning their own future. Even the captured Africans who jumped into the sea rather than be enslaved themselves made a decision.

Arvay notices this phenomenon in Black and white men on the waterfront calling back and forth to each other as they all head farther into the Atlantic. She sees the "boats pairing and falling in line" alongside the *Arvay Henson*. They stop and assemble like soldiers. A sandbar hampers their ability to move forward. A storm is coming. On the horizon, the thunder is getting "closer and louder all the time."[39] The wisest will wait until it is safe to continue.[40]

As they sit, a boat that is already out at sea approaches. The person piloting it, as Arvay will soon discover, is a "chestnut-colored Negro" who wants to talk to her husband.[41]

Anxious to hear what the man has to say, Jim jumps over onto the other fellow's deck. Arvay sees their hands moving mysteriously. Two Black fists hit each other rapidly.[42] Jim returns to her, smiling; they have agreed on something.

"Everything fast above and below?" Jim says to his two mates. After they make a final review, securing anything that can easily shift, he fixes "his eyes ahead," but the racially ambiguous mate warns Jim about the dangers.[43] Jim ignores him and presses on, holding his boat "on her course."[44] The ocean is full of danger, but he will have the final say. There are limits to sharing power. Indeed, since the ships are often named after their white owners, when something goes wrong, Black men "all cursed out the owners. . . . Did the fuel pump on the engine go bad? It was a Toomer, Meserve or whatever the owner's name so-and-so of a bastard! . . . Arvay found that Jim knew all about it, as did the other owners and laughed it off."[45] White men are able to laugh because in the end, they retain the most power. Or daring. Not even the threat of death seems to slow him down. Like Hurston, he pushes on. When the *Arvay Henson* heads into "grumbling and rumbling of the sea," it is not Jim but a crewman who is more terrified.[46] "Captain! My Captain! You gone crazy?" he asks. (Hurston's friends may have asked the same when she traipsed off to Honduras.) When Jim and even Arvay chastise him, he begins to cry and pray, stopping only when Jim orders him up and off his "rusty knees."[47]

Arvay soon discovers why Jim has put their lives at risk. This is her first visit to the sea. He wants her to see the sunrise. It is a "diffused pinkness" they would have missed had they remained back with the others.[48] "I thought you might like it, Arvay. Biggest thing that God ever made," Jim tells the woman who has left him twice.[49] But like water, which sometimes gets "stopped up," she finds her way home.[50]

His boat now circles as the hunt for shrimp begins.[51] The pelicans and seagulls swoop and swirl upon seeing the nets.

Jim and his mates catch turtles and other bycatch.[52] Has she jinxed the crew? If she has, Jim is not giving up: "There's shrimp in this goddamned ocean and we got to get 'em."[53] Because he is determined, they succeed. He and his crew catch and dehead their lot, putting most of it on ice.[54] Arvay takes the rest and prepares a meal of fried shrimp and other fixings in the galley.[55] As they return to the shore, she (and maybe even Hurston) now ask, "What more did she want than what she had already received?"[56]

Warner Bros. would someday give *Seraph on the Suwanee* a first and second reading. Jane Wyman, who had starred in *The Yearling*, the movie based on Rawlings's bestselling 1938 novel, was even considered for the lead role if *Seraph* got the green light.[57] But a "white trash" belle being abused by her husband was worrisome. Even if the white critics gave *Seraph* good reviews, many of Hurston's peers and fans were also skeptical, then and now. Years after her death, Alice Walker said Hurston had produced some white folks for whom it is "impossible" to care.[58] In short, when Hurston decided to make her lead character a pathetic trashy belle, she flopped.[59] But she was merely trying to fill the industry's needs;[60] producers were intrigued with stories about white folk, or "crackerphilia," well into the 1950s.[61] Aware of the market, Hurston tried to deliver. Hazel Carby has written that *Seraph* was her "most ambitious and experimental" work yet.[62] Hurston was, again, defying convention that said Black people could not write about white ones, if nothing else.

She was doing more, though. She set another book in Florida, a gateway between the so-called Old and New Worlds. St. Augustine, the country's oldest city founded by Europeans, is located there. But Florida is also a gateway to the rest of the Americas, which includes the land where the Mayans once lived. In searching for one of their ruins at the time she was also writing and revising *Seraph*, she tracked people living in two different civilizations. The Mayans demonstrated the

THE CHASE AND RUINS

possibilities on one side of the Atlantic before Europeans and Africans arrived. Before all the talk about who is Black and who is not.

*

Completing *Seraph* was also a means to an end. She wanted to find that Mayan ruin. She would go to a part of the country that had been heard about but not seen for about 200 years. "It is a forbidding area," she now told her editor. But she was not afraid of the jaguars, the pumas, or the rattlesnakes.[63] Some said the jungle to which she was headed was cursed. She was still going.

She had done her research on how the Mayan civilization had fallen. Crop failure was part of it. Outsiders, too. The Icaques lived in the mountains because they wanted nothing to do with intruders; their plan was to avoid the ones who brought disease and religion. She was the one to sort through it all. She was, after all, still from a people who had also suffered. She was not someone who had "the Blanco's eyes," or put simply, she was not white and thus not easily tricked by the Indigenous, who were strategizing how to improve the quality of their own lives.[64] While she was there, maybe she'd see two underground caves that the pre-Columbian Indigenous people built beneath their cities.[65] "So th[a]t is what I have in mind," she told her editor.[66] She wanted to ensure that he knew that she had big goals: not only *Seraph* but another book that foregrounded the Mayans. In either case, she most wanted a story to sell to a Hollywood studio.

If she had made it to the Mosquito Coast on the northeastern end of the country, she would have seen the mountains stretch down to the water. This is how one visitor who had been in the area nearly 100 years before remembered it.[67] At the time, a few roads allowed the passage of contraband when the Honduras fought Spain. By the mid-nineteenth century, foreign investments slowly began to trickle in. Construction on an interoceanic highway began in 1852 only to largely result in failure, just like the attempt to build a railroad in Guatemala that was supposed to connect that country to Mexico, Belize, and Honduras.

Still, the people continued to come, among them, researchers. Of great interest were the Indigenous groups whose presence in Honduras could be traced to at least 3000 BCE. John Lloyd Stephens, a lawyer from New Jersey, and Frederick Catherwood, an architect from London, were two of the earliest visitors to seriously document the lives of the Mayan people.[68] In 1839, Stephens and Catherwood traveled through Guatemala, Belize, Mexico, and Honduras. They claimed to have seen the ruins of as many as forty Mayan cities and determined that the people had had a highly developed society; particularly striking was their knack for mathematics, astronomy, art, and architecture. Their language had a musical monosyllabic sound and as many as 23 dialects.

The Mayans crossed the Bering Strait near Alaska looking for food 20,000 or so years ago. They headed toward Southern California, some getting as far as Chile.[69] Their decline, again, was traceable to a severe drought that began around 750 CE and lasted to as late as 1050 CE. Researchers have called this period the "Great Collapse." Widespread warfare and overpopulation also took a toll.

Even as scientists have debated how culturally unified Indigenous people in the Americas actually were, there are similarities between people in Mesoamerica and those in the southwestern United States.[70] The Mayans as well as the Aztec, Olmec, and Toltec people are collectively part of Mesoamerica's "high culture."[71] Some also lived in what is known as the highlands. Others lived in the lowlands. Some were more independent than others. The Mayans were thought to have traditionally confined themselves to a particular place in order to resist interlopers even though they traded from time to time with other groups. The Aztecs were among the ones to be avoided at all costs.

When Europeans began arriving on these coasts in the late fifteenth century, many Native people perished from disease. Those who survived were often enslaved like the Africans. When the British Empire outlawed slavery in the first half of the nineteenth century, arrangements were made for some enslavers to be financially compensated for their losses. John Potts, a lawyer in Belize, sought such a payment in 1829 from British government to compensate him for the value of several enslaved Native Americans who were freed in Honduras.[72] He and his sisters had inherited them from his father. Potts expected $100 apiece for the two least expensive ones, who were named Peggy and Sam. He expected $455 for the one whose name may explain the price: "Smart." Whether Smart was a man or woman is unclear.

In 1839, Thomas Young, an Englishman, traveled to the Mosquito Coast, the very place Hurston wanted to be. In a book published three years later, he announced the economic potential of Honduras. It would continue to be one of many Latin America countries to which foreigners want to flee, if the 1986 movie *The Mosquito Coast* and 2021 television series with the same name are any indication.[73] In both projects, dreamers relocate their families outside the States. They were on the run, too. Young himself wanted to reestablish a settlement that William Pitt, another Englishman, tried to build in 1732 located on the Black River, 80 miles from Trujillo. During his visit to Honduras, the Miskito people greatly challenged Pitt. By the time Young arrived, the locals were more agreeable. Speaking broken English, they presented him with bananas, pineapples, and sugarcane.

If Hurston had made it to the Mosquito Coast, she would have seen such fruit and glimpsed the tall and willowy coconut trees as well as the mangrove bushes whose branches stretched over the bay, leading into the Caribbean Sea.[74]

Young was most enchanted by the fragrance of lime trees. He wandered past thatched huts that sat as much as five to six feet from the ground where Miskitos slept in hammocks.

As he continued to survey the land, he also saw mahogany and cedar trees and other valuable things like the rich soil from which the Miskitos harvested corn and other crops, including sweet potatoes, ginger, and oranges. Their diet was supplemented by fishing and hunting. Young decided that he would make other Europeans aware of the natural resources of this "fine country" that with "the skill and perseverance of the white man" could be extracted.[75] Like many white foreigners of his day, he believed the Indigenous people that he met were lazy, the men in particular. He observed how the women, not the men, did the planting.[76] He also decided that disease had not wiped out their population. Alcoholism had.[77] He observed one minister use diluted rum to entice the Miskitos to listen to his sermons. The day he arrived without it, one of the Native chiefs departed, his people following.[78]

The Miskitos, in Young's best estimation, were different from the Black Caribs from St. Vincent. The Caribs could grow not only cassava, plantains, ginger, bananas, yams, rice, sweet potatoes, sugar cane, pumpkins, watermelons, but also black-eyed peas, Scotch bonnet peppers, and ingredients that reflected their West Indian and African past.[79] But to Young, the Caribs were not a "handsome race" even if their skin varied from "being coal black" to "as yellow as saffron."[80] Whatever beauty they lacked was compensated for by their work ethic; they were also "hardy and athletic," "scrupulously clean," and multilingual. Some could speak Carib, Spanish, English, "Creole-French," and even the Miskito's language. In a few generations, the Miskitos would be no more, he predicted.[81]

Young also encountered a French Creole woman in Trujillo who tended to him when he fell ill. She was jailed after trying to profit from a small vein of gold that her workmen discovered while digging a well behind her house.[82] The authorities wanted no part of mining there. Locals were, however, allowed to trade animal hides and indigo for hardware, cookware, and other manufactured goods.[83] Seeing the demand, merchants in Boston sent goods there every two or three months. Sea vessels arrived from Havana, Belize, and Guatemala, too.

In 1857, William Wells, a New Yorker, came to Honduras via San Francisco, visiting many places, including Olancho, a part of Honduras that is known today for its rampant violence. The region encompasses parts of the center and east of the country and is one of Honduras's largest departments, which may be thought of as states. There, gold was once so plentiful, Wells thought he was heading to "another California."[84] Before his departure, he interested, as he put it, several businessmen in his proposal to obtain permission to not only look for gold but export hides, timber, and other commodities from Olancho.[85] Over one year, he surveyed the many money-making opportunities. In his 1857 book, he declared that Honduras had "the vegetable and mineral wealth of New England and Virginia intensified ten-fold."[86]

While exploring the country, he befriended some of the locals by taking them roast chicken and fruit.[87] (Hurston did the same when she was conducting fieldwork, bringing food to the African who had survived his passage on the *Clotilda* in exchange for his memories.) From time to time, Wells observed the country's natural beauty, describing a stately pelican coasting, spreading its wings before dipping into the bay.[88] He also took note of the people who surfaced, not unlike Jim's mate in *Seraph*, as being little more than infantile. When a thunderstorm commenced, Wells watched one of his guides crouching in the boat like a "baboon."[89] When the squalls became too much and the rain came down, making it difficult to see, the other guides finally tried to adjust the sails.

It was too late. Water poured in. Wells watched his baggage floating with the other items from the boat.

The next day, Wells held a poncho around himself, still exhausted from the ordeal, and awakened the men around him.[90] He was ready to continue his journey but soon fell ill with a fever. A doctor tended to him, and for this he was grateful. He said the Hondurans believed the changes in the moon and the tide could have an impact on the severity of one's illness.[91] The less a foreigner had to do with the "quackery" of Central American medicinal practices, the better, he figured.[92]

As adventurers and investors continued coming to Honduras, more researchers arrived, too. Archaeologists and linguists in particular led the way, their numbers growing by the mid- to late nineteenth century.[93] Formal study of the region was undertaken in 1875 with the formation of the International Congress of Americanists to assess the history and cultures in the Americas prior to and since Columbus's arrival. In 1900, another conference was held in Paris to coincide with the World's Fair.

Many of the research teams that traveled to Central America well into the twentieth century had not only funding but project directors, surveyors, and other personnel that Hurston lacked. By 1950, the US Geological Survey made detailed maps of the remains of as many as 3,600 buildings in Mayapan, a Mayan site on the Yucatan Peninsula. These sites were difficult to find because of the country's dense vegetation. Still, in 1976, a British archaeologists reportedly located the oldest Mayan ruins in Central America's lowlands. Burned wood, jewels, tombs, clay, and plaster were among the artifacts discovered. Two years later, a second British group began fieldwork in the area with assistance from several North American researchers. In 1978, as many as 20 scientists, among them archaeologists from France, studied hieroglyphics at a Mayan ruin in western Honduras, near the Guatemalan border.

Despite lacking the support of other researchers, Hurston was determined to find the Mayan ruin. As she traveled to its approximate site on the northeast coast of the country, she would have initially passed swampy marshland as well as arable land used for growing coffee, bananas, tobacco, corn, and cotton that gave way to dense forests before seeing more open woodlands.[94] She could have used a rowboat, rail, and even a car for various legs of her journey. But the deeper she traveled into the jungle, the roads would have been unpaved, hindering further travel unless she was on foot or a mule. Indeed, she would have needed to rent such an animal and hire at least one muleteer.

Her use of a mule may have brought her a memory or two about *Mules and Men,* her 1935 book of southern African American folklore in which she linked the demoralizing labor of people of African descent and this overworked animal. While trying to reclaim their humanity as they worked, they'd became both "mules and men."[95] In *Their Eyes Were Watching God,* even Janie Mae, her Black protagonist, knew that being misunderstood went hand in hand with being a Black woman, the "mule uh de world."[96] Even if she sometimes wore blinders, Hurston had seen the horrors that the marginalized experienced. Even now she had the privilege of being curious about the Mayans and acting on her curiosity.

Depending on how far she got via mule, she would have also encountered scattered pine trees and locals wary of outsiders. There would be many lessons to learn in order to keep the people around her calm. She appears to have known some Spanish, which helped. She already understood that it was important to announce her presence to government officials, which helped, too. Someone in a high-ranking position surely knew she was on this side of the country. But as she traveled over land, she would need to secure landowners' consent before passing through their property. She would have done well to obtain a bit of favor by hiring locals who owned the land she crossed and, in light of the local politics, perhaps even people from several families living on or near the land.[97]

She would have bypassed some of the problems facing a male researcher in this country, who should have been wary of local women who wanted to marry a foreigner, as advertisements they placed in local newspapers made clear.[98] Such women had fathers and plenty of brothers that no smart man wanted to anger.[99] As an African American woman, if she wanted to have an affair, Hurston would have likewise had to be prudent. She was from the States, which made her appear exceptionally liberated, irking chauvinists in this country.

As was true in other countries she visited, the locals would have looked at her with great interest. She likely had to shoo people away. Marian Blumenschein, the wife of the doctor who built a clinic in Honduras in the late 1950s, certainly had.[100] A group of local women stopped speaking and dropped their washing to follow Marian when she left home to fill her water buckets. She took her place behind two small boys in a line of women and children waiting to do the same.[101] Some of the girls who held clay pots and galvanized buckets were not even 5 years old. As she waited, she heard the people around saying that she could not speak Spanish. She may not have spoken it, but she understood every word they said. She knew how to say *buenos tardes* in the afternoon rather than *buenos dias*.[102]

Some of the women wondered why she had not sent for her daughters to fetch the water. On the way back to her home, she slipped on pine needles. The next day, a teenager arrived at her door, asking if she wanted a local to do her laundry. Marian agreed, to spare herself the journey and the watching eyes.[103]

Like Marian and other foreign visitors, Hurston would have had to be mindful about the animals and reptiles she might encounter. Scorpions and tarantulas were ever present. She would have carried a stick to also shoo away snakes and dogs. If traveling on foot or by mule, crocodiles and jaguars were

THE CHASE AND RUINS

dangers, too. Cattle would have been uneasy about her coming near their calves. Poisonous plants were another concern. Being safe from people was doubtless on Hurston's mind, too. She had sometimes carried a gun while traveling through the US South. Central America had many things about which one should be frightened, too. Hurston herself would have to be wary of people. She discovered this very thing while trying to obtain photographs for her travel articles. Armed outlaws were more plentiful by the 1980s, but they were also present in the 1940s.[104] But she would have proceeded with the same courage seen in Stone, who, as one chronicler put it, was "hooked forever" while being out in the field, so much so, she returned repeatedly to "the land of snakes, jaguars and outlaws."[105]

CHAPTER FOUR

THE TWO WHO WERE DUPED BUT RESISTED EXPECTATION

Someone else had been down in Honduras. In many respects, her experiences uncannily paralleled Hurston's own, and thus she warrants some attention. María Soltera arrived in 1881.[1] During her nearly month-long stay, she probably saw some of the landscape that Hurston would encounter, even though several decades separated their visits.[2] The biggest transportation project in Honduras by the time Soltera arrived was the attempt on the part of the United States, Great Britain, and Honduras to build the interoceanic highway. The latter country's reputation for being swindled by outsiders likely began at this point, not with the banana plantations that foreign companies established there by the late nineteenth century. The first tremendous debt that Honduras assumed after its independence from Spain was connected to this rail project. Initiated in 1852, it failed by the 1870s even as some of the finished lines were leased in the 1880s to US businessmen. The Hondurans mostly blamed the British for the setbacks. When Soltera arrived in Honduras, a mule trail still ran near one hoped-for train line. By the time her adventures there were published by a university press in 1964, airplanes were flying over the still-unmarked path.[3]

She arrived in Central America on the eve of growing conversations concerning how bodies should be separated in public spaces in the States. Such discussions were pertinent even in Honduras, a country that would increasingly come under US oversight. That Hurston, an accomplished African American woman, was able to move freely in and outside of the States by the 1930s and 1940s was no small thing. That she did so as a citizen of a powerful nation was not either.

Soltera arrived in Honduras carrying, of course, the currency of her white skin as well as citizenship in a very influential country. She had other things in common with Hurston. They were both unmarried. Soltera, "single" or "spinster" in Spanish, was the pen name taken by Mary Lester. In keeping with the conventions of the travel writings produced in her day and earlier, she emphasized the exotic nature of the people and places she encountered, also reflected in her choice of pseudonym. Other Britons did similarly, some more egregiously than others.

The explorer Sir Richard Francis Burton is best known for translating *One Thousand and One Nights*, a collection of Middle Eastern and South Asian folktales, into English. His book was published in the same year Soltera arrived in Honduras, in fact. He disguised himself as an Islamic pilgrim while visiting Mecca; discovery that he was a European Christian would have resulted in his death.[4] His feat was so grand, Burton became a legend when he returned home. While visiting any number of impoverished communities, Hurston had basked in a different kind of privilege as an educated Black woman.

Soltera visited Puerto Cortés, the seaport on Honduras's northwest coast where Hurston would stay. She began her two-week, nearly 400-mile journey there from Amapala, the coast where Thomas Young, the explorer, had traveled. This town on the south side of Honduras sits on a gulf facing the Pacific Ocean. More than 50 years later, Hurston would use Puerto Cortés, essentially the seaport for San Pedro Sula, as a base before heading 400 miles east toward the fabled Mosquito Coast over which the British and Spanish once fought.[5]

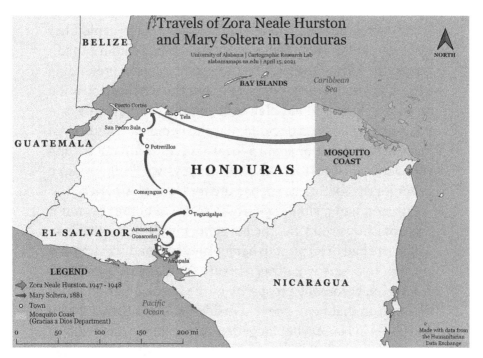

Zora Neale Hurston's travels in Honduras.
Courtesy of the University of Alabama Cartographic Lab.

There, she'd be nearer to the side of the Caribbean Sea that poured into the Atlantic.

The visits that both women made to the country were motivated by their desire to have financial security. Hurston, again, wanted to secure a Hollywood deal for the novel she wrote in Honduras or for a story involving a lost Indigenous ruin if her book didn't sell. Soltera hoped to secure a teaching job in a colony being established for British and Irish expats in San Pedro Sula, just over 30 miles inland from Puerto Cortés. As José I. Lara has written in his study of her exploitation of Victorian notions of white British womanhood, Soltera's trip was doomed from the outset because much of the information she received before her journey about her prospects was based on lies.[6] (The same may have been true for Hurston as well. Perhaps Brett, the English miner, and Irvine, the English captain, knew each other and had an undisclosed plan to exploit her research skills, if not the little money she had for an expedition on the Mosquito Coast.) A Protestant minister pretending to be a Catholic priest offered Soltera the teaching position on which she based her plan to spend the rest of her days in this colony. She even decided that she could earn additional income by playing organ in a local church. "I am not getting younger, and I want to make a home of my own," Soltera wrote in her journal before her departure for Central America.[7]

Hurston had a similar yearning to buy a home. Even if it was not a house on land, the houseboat in Daytona Beach on which she had lived prior to her journey to Honduras was one attempt to create what was a luxury for many people, Black and white, before the prosperity of the postwar period. Prior to living on that boat, she had resided at more than a dozen addresses in Harlem but longed to buy a cabin in Eau Gallie, a community on Florida's east coast, in present-day Melbourne. She'd been eying it since writing a book there in the late 1920s. Hurston wanted this cabin and other things while being well aware of the disappointments she routinely experienced personally and professionally and could continue to face as a Black woman.

She never denied the injustices that Black people faced; however, Hurston was not inclined to be visibly wounded by then. In fact, she learned how to minimize the impact of any letdown by remaining keenly aware of other matters before her. Even as the winds had blown and the rain had poured during that hurricane in Daytona Beach, she focused on writing letters to her contacts and on her determination to be in Honduras. In other settings, she regularly distracted herself from numerous discomforts by noticing the "interesting people" surrounding her. She had worked in St. Augustine in 1927.[8] Back then, she noticed such people, as she told one confidante, even though she was also feeling "a little lonely."[9] Two years after that trip, she was conducting research in the

Bahamas, recently divorced from her first husband, the University of Chicago medical student, feeling a "little depressed spiritually," as she told Hughes when they were still in regular contact.[10]

Soltera also felt lonesome in Honduras, declaring, "I am alone in the world."[11] As was true of Hurston, travel appears to have been one way that she eased some of her loneliness even if moving in such a manner brought other problems. She was visiting Honduras when the memory may have been still fresh for some locals of General Justo Rufino Barrios, Guatemala's president, and his attempt to head a reunited Central America. In 1841, the countries in this region dissolved the collective that they had formed after their 1821 independence from Spain. Marco Aurelio Soto, Honduras's president, had only recently stopped this latest of many uprisings in his country.[12] Some Hondurans were still reluctant to travel at night. That a white British woman was prepared to cross the mountains on the back end of such fighting was remarkable.

As was true of Hurston, Soltera knew how to be flexible while facing great difficulty. She was reportedly born to British parents in the Pyrenees but had lived in many places, including Australia and the Fiji Islands.[13] Like Hurston, Soltera knew how to manage physical discomforts. Both women were prepared to go hungry and make do with little money. Hurston once shared her delight in obtaining food during a research trip in Haiti: "I was very hungry and came upon a crowd of folks in a little town sitting around a pot of yellow corn mush seasoned with a little brown sugar. . . . I put down five cents. . . . My, my! It tasted so good!"[14]

There are obvious problems in making too much of what these two women have in common. Most of the evidence about their lives are words that they themselves produced on paper for a select audience. Hurston wrote letters to countless people. She evidently copied some of her correspondence because she was wary of most folks in her circle even if she made some of them laugh. During her time in Honduras, Soltera wrote entries in a journal that were initially intended for only her own eyes. Perhaps even then she knew that should her plans fail to materialize, she could sell her story. In 1884, three years after her visit to Honduras, she did just that. *Blackwood's Magazine*, a British publication, recast her journal entries in a five-part series. Not unlike Hurston, she could see possible hurdles, planning alternative uses for her work.

Soltera arrived in Honduras after recent technological advancements enabled people and products to move across great distances. She was in awe of how "the rail and steam . . . made the world . . . small enough" for her to move from place to place.[15] Leisure travel was a growing option for a select few as attitudes about where women should be and for how long loosened. She joined other women who had left the private sphere of the home for public spaces for several decades now.[16]

In 1827, just over fifty years before Soltera's journey to Honduras, Frances Trollope, another Englishwoman, salvaged a failed effort to open a bazaar in the States by recasting her own journal for publication. The result was a travelogue that, typical of the genre, featured her observations on the customs of people living in the United States, including the racial identity of the people she encountered. Voyage literature was a major genre for a more literate public by the seventeenth century, according to historian Andrew Lambert.[17] His own quest to discover why Englishmen were unwilling to relinquish tiny pieces of earth thousands of miles from their homeland led to a microstudy of the famed Robinson Crusoe Island. The island was the subject of a 1719 novel concerning a shipwrecked sailor on a tropical island near the coasts of Venezuela and Trinidad. The castaway's experiences seemed to have been inspired by a sailor shipwrecked on an island 400 miles west of Chile. Surviving records, published and otherwise, situated women in narratives involving the sea, real and imagined. Trollope herself approached the States on a passenger ship. Upon her arrival in New Orleans for the first time, she was struck by the large "proportion of blacks seen in the streets, all labour being performed by them; the grace and beauty of the elegant Quadroons," as well as the "wild and savage Indians."[18] A woman of her time, Trollope clearly could be as arrogant as other people writing travelogues who had even a bit of privilege in a modernizing world.

Eliza Potter, a New York native of African descent, shared her own striking views about the people she encountered as she traveled.[19] In *A Hairdresser's Experience in High Life*, a gossipy book published in 1859, Potter recounted her travels around the States, Paris, and England. As a biracial woman who earned a living largely as hairdresser and as a domestic serving the white elite, she heard and saw secrets of her employers as well as Black folks, which her narrative divulged. Potter recounted, for example, how many biracial women like her boldly advertised the advantages of their fair skin, which approximated white standards of beauty. Such women were particularly visible in Cincinnati, which sat on the Ohio River, the largest branch of the Mississippi, and had the country's highest per capita proportion of people of mixed race outside the South.[20] "In our Queen City of the West, I know of hundreds of mulattoes who are married to white men," said Potter, who had, like them, relocated to this growing metropolis, adding "and some ... are so independent they will be thought nothing but what they are."[21]

Louisa Picquet was also a biracial woman who moved to antebellum Cincinnati. She made her way there from New Orleans after being freed by her enslaver. Her 1861 travel narrative, published with the assistance of a white abolitionist minister, was just as preoccupied with race. Picquet recounted her chance meeting with a former lover she knew in Mobile who was passing for white in Brooklyn. He had produced two children with a white woman, but Picquet boldly pointed out one child's African features: "That one has the stain on it."[22]

Soltera was also quite attentive to the racial identities of the people she met as she traveled during the late nineteenth century. Sailing between Acapulco and Honduras, she referred to a servant as a "Chinaman."[23] She described an "enormous old lady of color" who needed assistance being "hoisted up the side" of the boat in one port town. After arriving in Amapala, Soltera watched a "black" man wade to shore with her luggage before returning to her boat and, with little warning, picking her up like she was a cat.[24] As she settled into her hotel, he even had the audacity to ask whether he could accompany her during her travels.[25] Having no shortage of confidence, he declared, "I as good as English."[26] A shocked Soltera yelled, causing the man to flee.[27] She later learned from the US consul in Amapala that this porter was known for his valor in three revolutions.[28] Locals called him "captain," in fact. This was hardly a word for a Black man whom whites did not respect. Upon learning this, Soltera continued to be haughty, declaring that her father was a military officer who had fought in Spain.[29]

*

Although she probably did not know as much, and if she did, possibly would not have cared, Antonio Maceo Grajales, a Cuban general, was in Honduras in 1881, the year she arrived. He descended from mixed-race Venezuelans who, during that country's struggle for independence, fled their homeland for the present-day Dominican Republic before moving on to Cuba, the very place Spain valued for its sugar production.[30] The demand for this commodity, however, grew alongside heartache for the nearly 400,000 enslaved people brought to Cuba between 1762 and 1838.[31] Hoping the island would someday be annexed to the United States, John Quincy Adams turned his head. Freedom for Africans in Cuba would harm slavery in the US South.

Having grown up in the countryside among the large sugar plantations, Maceo wanted to do something about the suffering of the enslaved. By 1868, he had already joined a group of anti-Spanish revolutionaries who were determined to rid Cuba of Spain. Some of these men were partly of African descent like the "captain" who offered Soltera assistance. Before the century ended, Maceo helped José Martí, the Cuban revolutionary. Maceo was known as the "Bronze Titan," not "Black Titan"; so pervasive was the hatred toward people with dark skin, some of his supporters could not bear hearing that he was part African:[32]

I have always denied and deny now that Maceo was a Negro, as many of the papers contend. That he was dark, I will admit, but it was a bronze-black from exposure—there was nothing of even mulatto in the fine, shapely head and fine forehead, the prominent arched nose, the thin, eloquent lips or the air of refinement with which he was ever surrounded.[33]

Despite what people said, Maceo identified with people of African descent in Cuba.[34] A tall, marble monument stands today in Havana in his honor. Not unlike Martí and Che Guevara, he had no use for imperialists. Maceo wanted to see equity in his homeland and elsewhere. Arturo Schomburg, a native of Puerto Rico, declared in the May 1931 issue of the *Crisis*, the official journal of the National Association for the Advancement of Colored People, that he knew of no military man who could "excel the exploits of Antonio Maceo."[35]

Like many public figures, Maceo was not a perfect hero. He had children with many mistresses even as he remained concerned about the well-being of his wife, Marie, who later relocated to Honduras to be with him. There, he obtained an appointment in the Honduran army.[36] While living in Puerto Cortés, he commanded that port as well as the one at Omoa. An accomplished guerilla fighter, he was quite invested in reforming the tactics used by the Honduran army. He was offering something that the Cubans, and people in Vietnam and other nations trying to rid themselves of Europeans, knew well: the art of guerilla warfare. In a slew of skirmishes in Cuba, Maceo showed courage, leadership, and skill fighting to liberate the enslaved and free Black peoples as well as the *guajiro*, or people living in the countryside, and even the *campesinos*, or peasants.[37] He would ultimately leave Honduras, however, following the political infighting that unfavorably positioned him against a colleague who supported Spain, the very country threatening Cuba's independence.[38]

No matter the feats of such a man, Soltera would still regard Maceo as a "Black" man and thus inferior to a white British subject like her. But she also had disdain for people from the States, not unlike Trollope and others. She doubtless felt lingering anger toward the once spoiled colonists who were despicable, save the occasional white American man who could be kind to lone females.[39] The captain of one of the ships on which she had traveled was such a "model American," a rarity in her mind.[40]

She was cautious with everyone on her travels, even people who wanted to help her. One man on the ship that brought her to Honduras gave her a revolver upon learning that she was sailing alone. He did not want to see her "get murdered" by the whites waiting to swindle even their own in Honduras.[41] No sooner had she accepted the gun, another man attempted to sweet-talk her out of it, teasing her about not knowing how to "fire it off," though he hurried away when another passenger saw the commotion.[42] With these experiences behind her, Soltera settled into her bed in the Amapala and rested before for her journey through the mountains.

The next morning, following the advice of an American consul, she hired as a guide Eduardo Alvarez, a young Honduran from Comayagua, a sizeable city between the south coast and San Pedro Sula.[43] But she was cautioned to keep an eye on him because he was "apt to be idle," like "all his race."[44] Soltera set out with him rowing her in a small boat. They headed to the open sea and soon turned into a narrow creek. They arrived in La Aceituna, where she slept in a hammock slung from the rafters of a customs house. White beans, grain, cowhide, and bales of coconut fiber were scattered on the dirt floor, an arrangement was that would compare favorably to the conditions of some of the area rooming houses she would encounter.

When the sun came up, she searched for a side saddle, which allows a woman wearing a skirt to modestly sit with her legs aside, rather than astride, a mule.[45] Using her "best Spanish," Soltera sorted through the offers from the villagers who were eager to profit from her.[46] She insisted that she would not pay more than 12 pesos. After picking her mule, she also rented one for baggage and hired Abel, another muleteer, who paced "with the regularity of a British sentinel."[47]

She and her two companions continued on and almost immediately faced their first delay. The mule carrying her luggage raced ahead, spilling everything. Her biscuits were ground into powder. Delayed by this mishap, they stayed in the town of Goascorán rather than continuing to Aramecina, their hoped-for destination.[48]

She took in the sights of the land and paid close attention to the conditions of the roads; those in Amapala were so unwelcoming, they were "what in courtesy must be called" roads.[49] O. Henry, Hurston, and the Blumenscheins determined the same. This was the case along the north coast plantations that the foreign fruit companies established at the turn of century. During Soltera's visit, paths like the one to Goascorán were particularly rough.[50] The friendliness of the people she encountered made up for the discomforts. An Italian shop-keeper, who was also a doctor, was especially kind. Soltera was given a comfortable bed in his general store. He was married to an Indigenous woman who had a "brown" baby.[51]

The only thing that worried her now was the conversation she'd had with a retired captain in the British merchant marine. He was a gruff man, who had little regard for their fellow countrymen who had swindled each other and the Hondurans trying to build the interoceanic railway.[52] However, when she awakened the next morning, she managed to enjoy the coffee and maize cakes brought to her. Afterward, the doctor suggested that she replace Eduardo with Marcos, another guide who was better in some unstated way, even if he also could not entirely be trusted either: he "dearly loves money" and would try to outsmart her.[53] She took this advice and hired Marcos, who offered her the use of Luisa, a gentler mule.[54] For now, he'd won her over.

Before she departed with Eduardo and her new guide, she took note of a fiesta the villagers were having and wandered around the town, attending mass at a tiny, "poorly furnished" village church.[55] The sight of the sun rising over mist-covered mountain peaks fortified her to continue her trip.[56] Before she left, the doctor's wife told her, "I shall never forget you," a show of affection Soltera considered "an outcome of woman's sympathy" over things neither of them could utter.[57]

Soltera and her guides finally headed into the mountains that figured into the origins of this country's name. Honduras means "great depths" when translated into English,[58] referring to the deep plunge from mountains into nearby waters and lowlands. "I am their daughter," Soltera said of these mountains.[59] She was energized by this new terrain. She and her guides made their way over difficult paths before taking the customary siesta. By seven that evening, they reached Aramecina, where she now hung her hammock in a public room. Her traveling rug and shawl offered needed privacy as she slept.[60]

She and the two men set out early the next morning, now facing sandy ridges that tested their mules' hooves.[61] Under rain and over marshy grassland they went, further challenging the mules' patience.[62] Upon reaching San Juan del Norte, their next stop, Soltera was so tired, she fainted. Surrounded by villagers, she came to after smelling a pungent brandy.[63]

A local woman offered her modest accommodations in yet another public room, but this time Soltera joined six other people, already sleeping in their own hammocks.[64] A candle with a nauseating smell kept away the mosquitoes.[65] As she had by now on several occasions, Soltera expressed her thanks with "a small gratuity."[66]

She and her guides continued on the following morning, encountering paths that were little more than loose stones, gravel, and dust. They soon headed into the highlands, facing rocks, potholes, and tree roots.[67] Their reward was a chance to drink from a stream. Soltera took advantage of an opportunity to bathe. A mass of bushes screened her as she undressed in the open air, deciding that it was no more immodest than European public bathing places like those in Brighton.[68] She and the two men then proceeded up the side of the mountain, and by evening, they placed her hammock in a public schoolroom. It was there that Marcos announced that he would not travel on to Comayagua unless she gave him money for beer. She refused, "determined not to be victimized."[69] Eduardo applauded her for being a "brave little lady."[70]

The next day, they crossed the San Juan River. She benefitted from the prayers of an elderly Indigenous woman who reminded Soltera of God's protection as they continued on to Comayagua.[71] At their next stop, Soltera enjoyed chicken stew offered by a Honduran couple on a farm.[72] She and her muleteers departed the following morning, encountering warmer weather as they made their way through the lowlands.[73]

The fluted tile roofs of Comayagua eventually came into view. "Madame Victorine," a Frenchwoman, her next host, provided a clean bed and a "luxurious" stewed pigeon and rice pudding.[74] Soltera's joys were short lived because she met a local bishop there, who announced there was simply no way she could obtain the promised teaching post. The government had not even fully sanctioned some matters related to the expat colony.[75] The bishop and her French host were also well acquainted with the questionable character of William Pope, the English minister who had enticed her to travel to Honduras. "You have not put any money into his hands, have you?" Madame Victorine asked pointedly.[76] Soltera declared that if any money were passing hands, it would be the minister reimbursing her travel expenses.

Angered, she rushed to send a telegraph to Pope to alert him to her arrival. She and her guides continued on to San Pedro Sula, staying in three more towns along the way. On the first evening of this final leg of her journey, she lodged in a "quiet and respectable house" owned by a poor widow.[77] As she and her guides traveled, they now crossed the River Blanco with the assistance of an Indigenous man who owned a canoe. After they reached Santa Isabel, a woman there offered Soltera "tough fowl" and tortillas.[78]

The next day, Soltera and her two guides continued, bothered now by a poisonous snake even though it passed without incident between the feet of one the mules. The mosquitoes were still an annoyance, particularly when the three slept under a full moon. Soltera found relief at an inn in Vera Cruz on the next leg of their journey. Grateful for what in the end was a pleasant stay, she gave her Spanish hostess some cotton print fabric to make a dress for her daughter.[79]

Soltera and her guides continued through a dell with a running stream. Next, they traveled on a rocky path before encountering a coyote that kept its distance and a cursed burial ground filled with stone sculptures.[80] She spent the

next evening in a shed offered by a family before they proceeded to the town of Potrerillos with a plan to take a train
the rest of the way to San Pedro Sula.[81] Marcos demanded to
be paid now so he could depart, as he had agreed only to get
her to the rail station in Potrerillos. She paid him and watched
him leave with Luisa, the mule that Soltera called "a tried
friend."[82]

Her woes continued. Typical of the country's transportation challenges, Soltera discovered that the rail line between
Potrerillos and San Pedro Sula, now just 50 miles away, was
in disrepair. After sleeping that evening in a small barn, she,
Eduardo, and Andreas, a new guide, journeyed on, entering
a rain forest that Hurston might have seen had she made it to
the Mosquito Coast. Soltera marveled at the "lovely, tangled,
uncultivated, damp" landscape, calling it "picturesque."[83]
Covered with greenery, they dodged a parasitic plant that
dangled, sometimes encircling them enough to lift them from
their mules.[84]

Next, they passed through more marsh, where they met
Pope, the minister who had conned Soltera. Beside him was
Jesus Gonzalez, the justice of the peace for San Pedro Sula.
Evidently intending to head off her allegations, Pope told
Soltera that he had not replied to her telegram because he had
hoped to reach Comayagua before she left, to spare her the
journey. Before hurrying away, he said he had made arrangements for her lodgings in San Pedro Sula on the chance that
they missed each other, something he evidently anticipated.
When she saw the filthy accommodations he had secured,
Soltera slept instead at an inn. A Creole woman told her she
had made "a long journey for nothing."[85] Pope even owed the
inn money. Soltera learned it would take as long as year to
receive an offer to teach in Honduras and decided to leave.
She waited two days for the next train to Puerto Cortés.

When she at last arrived on the north coast, Soltera decided that Puerto Cortés was "not much better than a sandy swamp, only waiting an opportunity to slip into the sea and be lost for ever as a human dwelling-place."[86] Its rail station was no more than a shed. Rusting bolts, rails, and chains, as well as abandoned tires, all remnants of the failed interoceanic railway, were strewn along it. The sandflies were "minute demons."[87] Although the town was on the sea, it was hardly a tropical paradise. Hurston likely thought the same, given her account of the moans in her hotel coming from "three señoras," almost certainly sex workers entertaining foreign businessmen, and the sounds booming from a construction site holding a Texaco storage tank.

Quite angry, Soltera visited the British consul in Puerto Cortés, who drafted an agreement that Pope should pay half of the money she had spent on the journey. She was certain that she would never receive anything from him. There, she waited an additional fourteen days for a ship heading to New Orleans.[88] By October 17, she left Honduras for New Orleans, arriving seven days later.[89]

Soltera traveled across several bodies of water and land, having survived something huge. She had traveled on her own to a foreign country. Hurston would do the same. Both women benefited from their ties to economically and politically powerful nations. They also carried liabilities, chief among them their own naivete. One believed she could find a ruin without personnel and funding. The other was duped by a con artist. They still accomplished something significant: they had resisted expectation.

As Lara has established, although lesser known than Trollope, Soltera joined other nineteenth-century white middle-class women travel writers in diversifying a genre initially dominated by men. Such women used their ability to move through space to showcase their competence as commentators on the many cultures surrounding them.[90] Such women without question participated in the process of empire building, too.[91] Some also affirmed the superiority of whiteness and femininity. Not only white women but biracial women like Picquet and Potter were surely sometimes compelled to embrace their own status as biracial women to better position themselves in a society that saw African Americans as inferior. (Hurston would, too, when she sorted through why she was most suited to find the Mayan ruin on the Mosquito Coast.) They, as had Soltera, created speed bumps for anyone unleashing too much judgment.

When she took a more difficult route over the mountains to San Pedro Sula, Soltera was not just pinching her pennies. She showed her readiness to embrace all kinds of discomforts. To be clear, she could have taken the rail from San Francisco to New Orleans to board a boat for a shorter journey to Puerto Cortés before heading about 30 miles inland via train to San Pedro Sula. She instead sailed from San Francisco to Acapulco before going to Amapala on the southern coast of Honduras. She apparently set aside Victorian notions that a woman needed to be spared from unnecessary distress.

She was audacious. She did not buckle upon discovering Pope's dishonesty. Hurston herself did not crumble after being swindled at least once, possibly twice, while writing freelance travel articles in Puerto Cortés to offset the cost of her stay in Honduras. They were two of a kind (Stone, the pioneering woman archaeologist who edited Soltera's adventures in the 1960s, was, too). Despite their disappointments, the trips to Honduras for both women seemed to have been worth it. Soltera, or Mary Lester, produced subsequent published writings.[92] Hurston returned to the States with an undisclosed accomplishment; she told her editor that down the road she "might have some interesting things" to share.[93]

*

Before her departure from Honduras, however, Hurston revised *Seraph*. As she wrote, the monotony of the rainy season did not go unnoticed. Her editor learned that if she was there another month or so, she'd be writing him "with a fin."[94] She saw as much as 18 inches of rain over three days in mid-January. Still, she was "fairly happy."[95] She longed to find the ruin and must have attempted another expedition or ran out of money and lodged elsewhere in the country, for the hotel was longer her return address.[96] She was receiving mail now at the Puerto Cortés office for the United Fruit Company.

By February, Hurston had booked passage on a ship home but experienced delays. She evidently failed to complete an unstated protocol. Given the length of her stay and her research agenda, she probably needed to share her progress. The authorities would have wanted to know whether she found the lost Mayan city she longed to see. If so, did she touch anything? After all, pillaging artifacts was prohibited.

To placate those watching her movements, Hurston traveled 33 miles from Puerto Cortés to San Pedro Sula to tend to what was likely a bureaucratic matter. She made four trips back and forth to San Pedro Sula and sent two telegrams to the minister of the exterior in Tegucigalpa, the country's capital. Although Honduras is typically regarded as a banana republic that was a puppet to foreigners, local authorities on the north coast apparently had sway, too.[97] If Hurston was briefly frustrated, she often remained humored. She remained arrogant, too, not unlike many other visitors. A 1959 report prepared by surveyors working for the British government used the following words about Belize, a neighboring country that, like Honduras, had its fair share of foreign presence:

We, the members of the team, who made this Survey, have derived great enjoyment from our task. Our team was representative of both the "Old Country" and newer countries of the Commonwealth, and, when the rain fell and the muddy trail seemed endless, we were sustained by the thought that we were working on behalf of a still younger member of the family; a country that needs technical and financial help as badly as any of the areas for which Britain has made herself responsible for progressive development.[98]

At the time these words were printed, Great Britain controlled Belize, which it would continue to hold until 1981. But there was no mention in this report of how Britain's earlier presence undermined the independence that the Indigenous people once had. The overall intent of this report was to instead determine how the land could be optimally further used as the Belizeans now pivoted to, as the British put it, "guide successfully the destiny of their own country."[99] In short, they must help themselves and clean up any mess that the outsiders made, sometimes with the assistance of well-positioned Central Americans. These British surveyors, indeed, referenced the "old heads" who might not have appreciated hearing any of this from the soon-to-be former colonizers whose financial coffers were too depleted by World War II to spare any resources to help the Belizeans.[100]

The position the British took in this instance was a far cry from their previous interest in this region. Nearly a century earlier, they were heavily invested in, among other things, controlling the outcome of relinquishing their oversight of the Bay Islands, which, like other countries in the Caribbean, had closer economic ties with the United States and even Belize than with Honduras.[101] When the Black Caribs, descendants of the Amazons and Africans who survived the wreckage of two slave ships in the mid-seventeenth century, were relocated to those islands, they proved troublesome to Great Britain's effort to become a leading producer of sugar on the island of St. Vincent. Some seventy years later, Royal Navy officer Alexander Milne led the world's most powerful naval force in monitoring the waters of the western Atlantic and Caribbean. While carrying out this mission, he was made aware of the ongoing difficulties with the transfer of power, and eventually handed over control of the Bay Islands near Truxillo, a Honduran port on that country's north coast, to the Hondurans.

By 1863, the former British residents who lived in the Bay Islands could be cantankerous, irking even their governor, Senior Francisco Bernardez. The English-speaking residents in Roatán, the largest of the Bay Islands, were unnerved about the difficulties in their government's effort to formally extract itself, at least on paper, from direct control of the islands. The locals reportedly "formed a body of Militia, and paraded the streets, with a Fiddle, Fife, and drum, hoisting a little Flag, and firing their muskets off continually in the air," causing the governor to "put up a proclamation, protesting against their arming themselves, without his authority."[102] For sure he and his countrymen knew that even while relinquishing control of the Bay Islands, the British government had a great ongoing interest in exploiting the financial possibilities of Honduras.

Ongoing interest in the country is evident in the hope of English and French people to establish an expat colony in San Pedro Sula, which they expressed in travel guides published for British tourists, among others. In the words of Commander Arthur Thrupp of the Royal Navy to his superior, Captain Peter Cracroft, which Milne was made aware of:

Though there is no immediate cause for anxiety for the British Interests at the Ports of Omoa and Truxillo, yet the future is still very obscure and doubtful, and many cruel murders, and great atrocities have been committed in the interior of the country, but I have not heard of any lately. Mr. [William] Melhado [the Acting British Consular Agent at Truxillo] fully intended sending a despatch [sic] by me, representing the state of the Country, and requesting that another man of War might visit Truxillo, to protect the interests of British Subjects.[103]

How far a war-weary and financially drained Great Britain had come by the mid-twentieth century that its interest in Belize dwindled.

Hurston was a citizen of a nation that also had much for which to answer in the aftermath of unwanted oversight of distant countries. She was also from a historically oppressed group and therefore experienced the contradictions of being on both the winning and losing end on many challenging matters. Even now, she claimed whatever privilege she could call up when she tried to save face for not having found the Mayan ruin. Her sojourn in "the bush" might require her to be tied to a shed until she was "house-broke again."[104]

CHAPTER FIVE

HEALING IN MIAMI BEFORE A FAILED RETURN

Within seven months of her return to the States, Hurston was arrested in New York on charges that she had molested an underaged Harlem boy. "I have resolved to die," she told Van Vechten and his wife, Fania Marinoff.[1] Hurston wore a red scarf to her preliminary hearing, signaling the Haitian practice of inviting the protection of Ogun, the warrior god.[2] She was most angered by a Black newspaper in Baltimore running a story about her arrest. An African American court employee leaked the story.

Six months passed and the charges were dropped. She was in Honduras when the assault was alleged to have occurred. She chalked the ordeal up to having angered Richard Rochester, a white fellow Republican with whom she became acquainted while she was working in Los Angeles, hoping to make it big in Hollywood.[3] In 1946, she and Rochester campaigned for Grant Reynolds in his unsuccessful bid for a US Senate seat. Democrat Adam Clayton Powell Jr., son of a well-regarded Harlem minister and community activist, prevailed. Powell's win was not what drove the wedge between Hurston and Rochester, however. Hurston said it was because she refused to lie for him in a small claims case involving a car. He retaliated by reaching out to the mother of a child Hurston knew, a Columbia University employee and her former landlord with whom she had exchanged words. Before Hurston left for Honduras, she'd made some suggestions concerning how the woman could obtain assistance for her child's disconcerting behavior. This child may have been on her mind when she wrote about the mentally challenged and soon dead son of Arvay, the protagonist in *Seraph*.[4]

Some have said this ordeal was the beginning of the end for Hurston, who began to act erratically.[5] Perhaps because she had overidentified with the privilege attending US citizens while in Honduras, she shaped her pain as a betrayal committed not only by Black people but by the United States. "My race and my nation have seen fit to befoul me with no excuse whatsoever," she told Fannie Hurst, the novelist who had befriended her early on during her days in Harlem.[6] "My country has failed me utterly," she also told Van Vechten and Marinoff, adding:

> My race has seen fit to destroy me without reason, and with the vilest tools conceived of by man so far. A Society, eminently Christian, and supposedly devoted to super-decency, has gone so far from it's [*sic*] announced purpose, not to protect children, but to exploit the gruesome fancies of a pathological case and do this thing to human decency. Please do not forget this thing was not done in the South, but in the so-called North. Where shall I look in this country for justice? This has happened to me, who has always believed in the essential and eventual rightness of my country.[7]

She had been a foreigner. She was Black. She was also American. Who was going to mess with that? Apparently someone had. Recall that she had experienced rejection by some of her more progressive her peers in Harlem now for several years.

To heal from the lies about her touching somebody's child, she reached out to—of all people—Irvine, the British boat captain who had earlier failed to take her to Honduras. They would now leave on the *Challenger*, another schooner.[8] In July 1949, she and Irvine traveled first to the Bahamas. Hurston turned to her writing to distract herself.[9] It was around this time she decided to salvage any memory she could from her earlier time in Honduras. The result was the beginnings of *The Lives of Barney Turk*, a novel in which a white male adventurer embarks from Florida to Honduras. If she couldn't go back to Honduras, he could. And like Hurston, he hoped to make it big in Hollywood. She'd get to Hollywood via a white man.

She worked on this story while Irvine turned back from the Bahamas for Miami Beach. He apparently hoped to pick up some cargo there to cover the cost of their travel to Honduras. He seems to have spent more time visiting the horse track, where he gambled away his money, and possibly whatever she had, too. Short on cash, he must have finally started seriously looking for a client who needed cargo hauled to Central America. They waited, moored at a pier near the MacArthur Causeway, close to the 13th Street Bridge on Miami Beach.

While there, Spanish-speaking marines mistook Hurston for a foreigner. As she told Mitchell, her editor:

> It is a joke, but here in Miami I have had to insist on remaining Colored. Somehow, everybody along the waterfront tries to make me out Cuban or Mexican. I suppose that started from the fact that two Argentine Vessels [*sic*] the *Don Guillermo* and the *Josefina Marina* are berthed next to the *Challenger*, and both outfits used to come aboard to talk Spanish with me.[10]

Her words suggest that her prior unhappiness about Irvine's desire to bring along a traveling companion to Honduras was tied as much to the woman's politics as it might have been to some unstated relationship between him and Hurston.

Zora Neale Hurston's travels in Florida and Miami.
Courtesy of the University of Alabama Cartographic Lab.

Irvine's present unhappiness might indicate they had shared an intimate moment: he did not like Hurston talking to the Spanish-speaking mariners. She was not a woman who seemed to have ever ruled out having a romantic tryst under the right circumstances. Before she left Daytona Beach, she wrote about the "good looking" men down in Honduras who were "plenty willing."[11] She indicated to her editor that the near-universal image of Latina and Black women being

THE CHASE AND RUINS

sexual and promiscuous creatures was the furthest thing from her mind.[12]

Perhaps she'd had a fling while visiting in 1930. In this particular instance, maybe Irvine simply did not want her talking to the men on the boats beside them because she and those men were all speaking Spanish, a language he could not understand. Either way, after he forbade her to speak to these men again, the conversations soon ended. Because she needed passage to Honduras, she did not complain about it either.

Hurston now passed the time in a nearby park, where she attempted to eat fruit from a sapodilla tree. She would have to work, "to fight, for it," as she told her book editor, because "Miami does not prohibit the people from eating the fruits in the public parks, and every day, some viper is around that sapodilla tree beating me to the ripe ones."[13]

She eventually learned the *Challenger* "was nowhere near ready to sail," as she had been led to believe.[14] Disappointed herself, Irvine became frenzied and wanted her company to calm himself from another evidently failed love affair. His request was an imposition, as she had her own worries. She may have found solace in observing her surroundings. "The traffic pouring to and from Miami Beach makes a steady drone from dawn till nearly dawn again," she told her editor.[15] Despite her problems, she could still look "dead across the bay" to see "Miami's well-advertised skyline."[16] Hemingway had Havana and Key West. Hurston had Honduras and Miami, among other places. The sky most enchanted her while she was in Miami. "God keeps His appointment with Miami every sundown. Berthed on the east of Biscayne Bay, I can look to the western side. . . . It is just too marvelous," she told her editor.[17] She adored the peninsula and once declared that she "loved sunshine the way it is done" in Florida. "I dislike cold weather and all of its kinfolk," she added cheekily.[18]

*

The city's beginnings could be traced to Julia Tuttle, a newly widowed white woman from Cleveland who bought 640 acres hugging the north bank of a waterway that is now called the Miami River. Tuttle herself had prime real estate, but she was willing to share some of it. Even after the winter freezes of 1895 and 1896, Black and white people continued to come to the city that became known as Miami. Tuttle, Flora Mac-Farlane, Isadore Cohen, William and Mary Brickell, Joseph Parrott and James E. Ingraham, the Peacocks, Sears, Sewells, and Burdines, and Ralph Munroe are names often mentioned in the story of city's beginnings. Less heard are the names of people of African descent who ensured the city's founding. When Miami was incorporated, 162 of the nearly 400 voters needed to incorporate the city were people of African descent, one of whom, Silas Austin, was the first name on the charter, in fact.[19]

A rail line owned by Henry Flagler, a rich New Yorker, brought the trains that jumpstarted the area's tourist economy and the city's position as a gateway to the rest of the Americas and even the world. Carl Fisher, an Indiana realtor, developed the barrier island east of Miami where Hurston now sat on the *Challenger*. He had big ideas for the place that was soon named Miami Beach.[20] Part of this six-mile-long stretch had been used for an avocado plantation.[21] Few knew why Fisher wanted to further develop "this ribbon of a swamp" covered in mosquitoes, pines, and palms.[22] Fisher had seen Atlantic City and decided that he could bring waterfront tourism down there, too. With the help of mules and horse teams, steam shovels, engineers, and Black laborers, he filled in the swamps with sand dredged from the bay's floor. By 1915, Miami Beach was incorporated. After a slow start, the people came. When Fisher extended the Dixie Highway from Michigan to Miami in 1927, their numbers grew.

Hurston had seen the tourists, but she'd had enough. It would take a while before she could leave, though. She sent letters from five other addresses in the area during her eight-month stay in a place she had planned to be, but only for so long.[23] As was possibly true during her time in Honduras, she had severe income and housing problems. She moved from one dwelling to another in a segregated tourist city.

Nearly half of the tourists said they came to Miami for the climate.[24] More than half arrived by car and a good many of the rest by train.[25] Some stayed in Miami where the year-round population was now half a million. Others traveled on to Havana, Nassau, Kingston, and elsewhere.[26] Black Miamians and their white allies saw the uneven distribution of wealth and set out to address the social inequity that permitted some, but not all, to vacation in this manner.[27] People of African descent who worked in hotel laundry rooms and port shipyards began attending rallies as early as 1943 to address inequities in the local tourism sector. Within a year, Pan-American World Airways was founded as an integrated organization.[28] By 1963, Harry Belafonte broke the color line by staying at the Eden Roc, a Miami Beach hotel. Before then, many postwar Black tourists stayed at the Hampton House, a motel that hosted many legends, including the Reverend Dr. Martin Luther King Jr.[29] Advertised in Black newspapers throughout the country when it opened in 1961, this hotel's amenities included a fashionable lounge featuring nightclub acts, meeting rooms, a convention hall, and a swimming pool encircled by tropical foliage. As chronicled in the 2020 Regina King film *One Night in Miami*, while lodging there, Malcolm X counseled a boxer who was then named Cassius Clay before his historic 1964 fight on Miami Beach against Sonny Liston.[30]

Even if they were still living in segregated conditions, Black folks in South Florida were in a sunny place, something Hurston appreciated even while in Honduras. She considered returning to New York, but she remembered a song with this warning: "Baby, it's cold up there."[31] Seeing few options, Hurston's next stop was the home of George Smathers, a white moderate who lived with his wife on a large lot close to the bay, just north of Miami's downtown. Nearby was a causeway named for Tuttle before the city was founded. Hurston's arrival in the Smatherses' home was timely. He was making a primary bid for a Democratic US Senate seat. Claude Pepper, his opponent, was a member of Florida's House of Representatives and later a US senator. Pepper had much to say about Truman's second bid for the White House in 1948. Truman sent Smathers his way: "I want you to beat that son-of-a-bitch Claude Pepper," and he did just that.[32]

When she campaigned for Smathers, Hurston had a front row seat to the rise of the Right. With Truman's backing, Smathers steered clear of the Dixiecrat revolt in response to Truman's decision to integrate military.[33] Race matters should be left to the states and not the federal government, Smathers decided. That said, he could make something of how Pepper had supported a bill trying to stop a half-million dollars from going to the commission created under pressure in 1941 to prevent discrimination in the defense industry, even if Pepper said he supported the measure only because the country was at war.[34]

Seeing Smathers coming after him, Pepper bragged in rural Florida about being a native Alabaman who'd spent the past twenty-five years in Tallahassee. Smathers was a newcomer, a young lawyer from New Jersey.[35] In the end, Pepper had the more enduring legacy, not Smathers, who died in 2007 largely forgotten.[36] Although Pepper once offered to post bail for Martin Luther King if he promised to leave St. Augustine, he also supported Social Security, Medicare, and Medicaid, programs that helped Black and white constituents. Elderly people were among his biggest supporters.

He and Smathers, however, both made political headway during a time when many white men thought their country had been snatched away from them. They believed the socialists, communists, and intellectuals were overwhelming what

THE CHASE AND RUINS

they believed were traditional "American" ideals.[37] They were not the only ones irked. "These do be times that take all of what you have," Hurston herself told one confidante in 1944, the year she yearned to return to Honduras and finally began making preparations for what in the end would be an eight-month stay. "I do not refer to the battlefields, but to this enormous pest of hate that is rotting men's souls," she told Benjamin Botkin, who worked in the Folklore Division of the Library of Congress and before that had been a director of the Federal Writers' Project. "When will people learn that you cannot quarantine hate? . . . I see it all around me every day. I am not talking of race hatred. Just hate. Everybody is at it."[38]

But openings existed for people to reach across the color line, as she herself discovered even now. In 1950, the year she campaigned for Smathers, she also helped Sara Lee Creech, a white human rights activist in Central Florida. Creech wanted to make an anthropologically correct doll that didn't demean the physical features of African Americans. Creech delivered. A happy Hurston told Creech, "The thing that pleased me most . . . was that you, a White girl, should have seen into our hearts so clearly, and sought to meet our longing for understanding of us as we really are, and not as some would have us."[39]

Hurston was not alone in her complex disposition. Ayad Akhtar, the Pulitzer Prize–winning writer, saw his father wrestle with his devotion to the United States in a semiautobiographical story of a Muslim man with ancestral ties to Pakistan who fawns over Donald Trump, one of his former patients.[40] He felt so close to Trump that he had withdrawal symptoms when he stopped treating the man who would become the president of the United States. So devoted was his father to Trump, he registered for obscure conferences in New York to have the opportunity to rekindle the memory of staying in a fancy suite on a Trump property, where Trump had earlier covered the cost of his stay. Akhtar's father would also visit Brooklyn to see a tailor who happily welcomed him for having been Trump's doctor.

His father and Trump made bad business moves. Akhtar's father had worked as a cardiologist at a teaching institution before building a private practice. Bored, he took a real estate seminar held one weekend at a Radisson Hotel in West Allis, Wisconsin. To celebrate his purchase of a gas station, he made a pitcher of *lassi*, a rose-flavored Indian yogurt and fruit drink. He went on to invest in a strip mall, a campground, a trout farm, and other ventures. When the 1987 stock market crash led to his financial ruin, he sold his practice to pay his debts. His son took out student loans to pay his college tuition while his father returned to teaching in an academic setting. This career move resulted in awards and a breakthrough discovery in irregular heartbeats, the very health condition with which Trump had struggled.

Akhtar's immigrant father was devoted to someone who "doesn't really mean" what he says about Mexican immigrants, and besides, "these people need to learn English."[41] He also heard his father say, "I don't pray; I don't fast; I'm basically not Muslim; you're the same; he's not talking about us. And anyway, I was his doctor, so we don't have anything to worry about."[42] Trump was just part of a "new era of political truth telling."[43]

Akhtar himself was born on Staten Island. He'd earlier written a play featuring an American-born Muslim who is aggrieved but also committed to his country.[44] When asked whether he felt a bit of pride on September 11, 2001, the day "America deserved what it got," he understood that people were really inquiring about where he stood on 9/11.[45] He allowed only this: the play came from somewhere. It is a combination of things that are complex and contradictory. Hurston was also complex and contradictory. Her adoration of and time spent in Honduras and elsewhere, including Miami, more than demonstrated as much. She was Black. She was a woman. But she was also an American. She was not unlike Syd (Gabrielle Union), the African American Drug Enforcement Agency detective in the 2003 motion picture *Bad Boys II*, a sequel to a popular 1995 film about two African American narcotics detectives in Miami (Martin Lawrence and Will Smith). Hector Juan Carlos "Johnny" Tapia (Jordi Mollá), a merciless Cuban drug dealer, kidnaps Syd, the sister of one of the detectives, and whisks her away to Cuba. When she is in Miami, Syd is "Black." In Cuba, she is "American." Tapia and his mother pasted these labels on her in a way that speaks volumes about the fluidity in American and African American identity.

Like Hurston and the African American military officer killed in 1907 in Honduras by a Nicaraguan, Syd is a member of a historically oppressed group. She is also a citizen of one of the most powerful countries in the world. She must be protected. An eclectic team of law enforcement officers and former military men, among them Cubans, arrive in Havana to save her. But she also saves herself by circumventing land mines at the Guantanamo base. It is Syd who sets off a mine explosion that kills Tapia. Like Hurston, tired or not, she participates in ensuring her own survival.

*

However, Hurston was surprisingly unhappy with a pivotal change in her own country's history. On the issue of the 1954 Supreme Court *Brown* ruling outlawing segregation in public spaces, for which she had no use, Hurston had said only what the Black nationalists would later say: Black folks could take care of their own. The artists, poets, dramatists, and others participating in the Black Arts movement in the 1960s and 1970s and the professors writing the lesson plans for the newly created women's studies and Black studies programs passed her by. Some may have been aware of her support for Spessard Holland, Florida's governor between 1941 and 1945 and a US senator from 1946 to 1971. In a 1950 letter to Mitchell, her editor at Scribner's, she proudly boasted about the "real conditions in the South," where some lawmakers sought answers "more earnestly than the on-lookers from above the Mason-Dixon line."[46] She remembered Holland's ample library and his books about "the Negro from way back before the war between the states. I saw them and envied him."[47]

Her steadfast disregard for liberals and even northerners is also seen in a letter she sent Holland's wife, Mary—whom she reverently called "Miz Mary." In 1958, two years before her death, Hurston mocked Pepper, who still aspired to office in Washington, DC, and only clinched a seat in Miami after the Cubans left their homeland in large enough numbers to result in the creation of a new district. He snagged it even though he had been a fervent New Dealer, or liberal, which is to say, the very thing some of these newcomers despised.

Even if this era gave Black people access to government programs, the liberals and the communists alike used them as pawns, she decided. Hurston reported taking the time to speak to small groups of African Americans to remind them that Miz Mary's husband was "the father of Negro education in Florida, and that it is always preferable to see a promise any day than to hear about one, and that Pepper had not[h]ing to show but words and weasley [sic] words at that."[48]

During the 1950 Smathers-Pepper race, African Americans were reportedly paid a dollar a vote. Since they voted overwhelmingly for Pepper, at least one scholar has surmised that the Pepper campaign may have been as "fully engaged in such practices as was the Smathers campaign."[49] Was she aware of this? If she was, had she easily worn the lapel pin reading, "ELECT GEORGE SMATHERS UNITED STATES SENATOR"?[50] Had she followed the injunction to be on the "alert to pick up any Pepper brochures, handouts, cards, etc., and send it all to State Headquarters"?[51] Was she privy to the instructions to give consideration to "methods of contacting the negroes in an effort to [sic] campaign workers" to influence their votes?[52] Had she witnessed white ministers working as closely as African American and white war veterans to help her candidate?[53] Without knowing the answers to these questions, one can be more certain that she made money while watching it all, as she had while cleaning Rawlings's house for ten days and later writing an essay about being a "Negro" pet. An essay she wrote for the November 1950 issue of *American Legion* had this headline: "I Saw Negro Votes Peddled."[54] In this article, she downplayed her reason for being in Miami: It was not because she was stranded there after being duped once more by Irvine. Rather, she came down after being made aware that someone from the "north" was heading to the state of Florida to influence the Black vote. It was then that she made up her "mind to be in Florida."[55]

But did Hurston know that African American voters in Florida dropped from 44 percent to almost half that number in 1950, the year she was helping Smathers?[56] That same year she gave a talk on his behalf at St. Paul AME Church in Miami's Liberty City, a historically African American neighborhood. Gloria "Gigi" Braynon Watson, the late public school French teacher and a dear friend of mine, attended this church in the 1950s. Did she and other members of her prominent and respected family—they owned two grocery stories and a pharmacy, the latter because their daughter who was a pharmacist couldn't get a job in any Miami drug store—see Hurston on this day? Did any of my people see her stomping the sidewalks of Miami's Black communities for Smathers? By then, Black folk were plenty tired. They lived in a country that told someone who would be shortly three-fifths of a person to go after the red coats and next, the blue and gray coats, and when you're done, liberate Europe. Chase the Viet Cong. Nina Simone sang in 1971 at Ft. Dix, "You got to get me through this mess."[57] In 1968, more than half of the people slaughtered in the My Lai Massacre in South Vietnam were babies.[58] The

HEAR

Rev. R. A. Jackson

Pastor of St. Paul A.M.E. Church

And

Miss Zora Neal Hurston

FAMOUS NEGRO AUTHOR

Sun., April 30, 3p.m.

Over Station WWPB

(Immediately after the Southland Singers)

In behalf of the candidacy of

Geo. A. Smathers

FOR U. S. SENATOR

Paid Political Advertisement

George Smathers paid political advertisement for Zora Neale Hurston's talk in Liberty City Church.
Miami Times, April 29, 1950.

lead executioner was a US Army second lieutenant who was nearly a child himself. Sentenced to life in prison for a massacre the army kept quiet until the media relayed the news, he said he only did what he was trained to do: kill.[59]

In Florida, Black folk strove for the promises of citizenship by fighting back in another kind of way. In Jacksonville there was a "knock down and drag out" brawl in an 1885 meeting as Black people there attempted to participate in local politics.[60] Five years later, Black farmers in Ocala hosted a national convention for Populists. The scores of African American men who served during the Civil War, some as noncommissioned officers, spoke their minds.[61] But not even two months after the Civil War ended, a newspaper editor in Gainesville said the country was still going to be run with "a government of WHITE MEN."[62] He was as unwilling as other whites to accept the degree to which African Americans weren't going to go down easy. At the time, Harrison Reed lured African American voters with promises, becoming Florida's governor.[63] He went on to veto a law to give Black people equal access to railroads and public accommodations, and yet 50 African Americans were among the 82 delegates attending the state's first Republican convention.[64] Some of them even backed a former enslaver over a Northerner for one position. Regional loyalty can be thick in the US South. Black folks' political awareness was partly owed to their beginnings in South Carolina, a state that had a large population of free people of color with ties to the Caribbean. There, people often identified on the basis of where they were from rather than on the basis of skin color.

As Bahamians arrived, often via the Keys, looking for work alongside the descendants of Cubans and Spaniards, some became lawyers and teachers.[65] Freewheeling capitalism began on the country's southernmost border.[66] Some people of African descent stood beside white ship captains deliberately wrecking sea vessels to collect the insurance money.[67] The familiar horrors continued. The 1923 massacre of African Americans in Rosewood followed an alleged rape of a white woman by an African American man. In 1934, a Black farmhand in Marianna, in the panhandle, was lynched following accusations that he raped and murdered a white woman.[68] Franklin Roosevelt asked for a federal investigation but later decided it was not worth alienating the southern voters who had the Democratic majority in Congress. No charges were ever filed in connection to the farmhand's death. Hurston had seen how he could care and not care despite his "new deals."

The degradation that African Americans in Florida faced was especially visible in the sawmill, turpentine, and other industries that she knew well. Her writings on these issues remain some of the most authoritative.[69] Even as the hopeless left for northern cities, the Miami chapter of the NAACP was anything but moderate. When asked to give up a list of names of its members to a state committee bent on identifying communists, Father Theodore Gibson, a native Miamian of Bahamian descent and president of Miami's NAACP, said no. Gibson was descended from Caribbean people who often said no. During the nineteenth century, Milne, the British admiral, wrote to his brother in Scotland of witnessing especially defiant Jamaican laborers: "They get up at 7 o'clock . . . and at 12 they throw down their hoe[s] and say, 'There's 15 pence I work no more this day['] and most probably will not work for 2 days to come."[70]

By the mid-1940s, the Ku Klux Klan became increasingly active in South Florida. Concessions were made following the 1945 "wade-in" at Haulover Beach, which led to the Black community getting its own beach.[71] Meanwhile, white Jewish radicals who relocated from the northeast to Miami recruited Black men from street corners, pool rooms, and barber shops for sit-ins.[72] Shirley Zoloth recalled being called a "nigger lover" and "dirty kike" at the downtown Woolworth.[73]

All of this history also lurked behind Hurston's support of Smathers. Something else did, too. Not unlike many immigrants to the States, she had often been able to self-identify on the basis of her ties to her initial origins, which is to say, her upbringing in an all-Black town. She could see the injustices that her people had experienced as well as other ways that Black folk could be defined. Persecuted or not, they were US citizens, self-sufficient in the way Booker T. Washington imagined even as he received flak. This realization took on new meaning during her travels abroad. She was Black but also a citizen of one of the most influential countries in the world. As pitifully arrogant and greedy as her country could be, that was something on which to sometimes hold.

While working for Smathers, she also assisted his father, Frank, a judge, with his memoir. She apparently charmed him as much as she charmed other whites. In an undated letter, perhaps one sent after she left Miami in 1950, the elder Smathers mentioned Ernest Hemingway's *Old Man and the Sea*. In an undated telegram, he asked, "When are you coming down? Will only be here two weeks. Hurry along. Judge Frank Smathers."[74] His wife, daughter of a Florida pioneer who had served in the Confederate army, sent Hurston a box of mangoes.[75] The letter accompanying this gift included "every good wish" for her "success."[76] Perhaps even the Smatherses had learned that she wanted to sell a story to Hollywood. However, friendships maintained via mail and ones maintained in person are two very different things. While working for Frank, Hurston said she would not put up with the cranky elder who "stuck his crippled fingers in his ears" so as to not hear her. She once "reached over and pulled them out and kept on talking."[77]

A 1927 map of Miami shows the Smatherses' house constructed on a lot that had a two-story dwelling to its rear, which may have been a parking garage with a guest apartment on the second floor. She possibly slept there and took breaks from working by walking to the end of the road to stand beside the bay. In that direction she could see where she was headed next. Perhaps with the assistance of someone living in the Smatherses' house—maybe a Black housekeeper—Hurston found work next as a maid in Rivo Alto, a tiny Miami Beach community on one of the six artificial islands not far from the dock where Irvine's ship was moored. The islands were connected by a Venetian causeway that ran between Miami Beach and Miami.[78] Built in 1937, the causeway had arched bridges designed to evoke Venice, Italy. Prospective buyers of the lots on Rivo Alto and islands near it were unconcerned about the Great Depression. This land was in such high demand, it was sold while some of the lots were still underwater.

The house she cleaned was ample, with a bathroom off each of its three bedrooms. There, she had another view of the bay as well as sunrises and sunsets. She may have been a maid, but she had access to the area's natural beauty in a city where racial progress was still slow in coming. Burdines, a department store chain in Florida, targeted seasonal white readers. However, some of the advertisements in the *Miami Herald* featured illustrations of white and Black girls in dresses announcing the coming Easter holiday as well as an African American woman in resort wear.[79] The same pages of the *Herald* announced that the Miami county commission unanimously approved a slum clearance initiative. Still, Elizabeth Virrick, the white civic leader empathetic to the plight of Black Miamians, declared the plan was "nothing but a hodge-podge if it is ever accomplished."[80] Black Miamians living in desperate conditions could not, after all, sit at the lunch counter at the Burdines downtown store.[81]

Hurston's training as an anthropologist might have allowed her to share her take on the social issues in Miami and beyond, but nothing of the sort made it into an article written by James Lyons, a young writer for the *Miami Herald*, who wrote a story about her working as a maid in Rivo Alto. After apparently reading a *Saturday Evening Post* article written by Hurston, her employer—a southerner—discovered her maid was an acclaimed author and anthropologist.[82] "It was a difficult few hours," her boss told Lyons. "But I must say without reservation that Zora is one of the most cultured and amazing women I have met and surely one of the finest. You just have to like her."[83]

Hurston said she only took the job to gather research for a project on domestic workers.[84] She offered other reasons for her presence in this woman's home: "I was born with a skillet in my hands," Hurston said. "I like to cook and keep house. Why shouldn't I do it for somebody else a while? A writer has to stop writing every now and then and just live a little."[85]

When the article was published, she was revealed as the accomplished woman she in fact was by this time. The titles of her published books were included, as well as her cowriting credit on a collection of Bahamian folk songs with African American composer William Grant Still, her attempts to write for Paramount studios in Hollywood, and her memberships in the American Folklore Society and Zeta Phi Beta sorority, as well as her Guggenheim (she had earned two by now). Her sale of her "Daytona Beach houseboat" to fund that year-long expedition into Honduras was reported as well. She was "not exactly affluent on her return a few months ago," Lyons observed, explaining her career shift to housekeeping.[86]

Hurston skillfully shifted the facts as she had for years when she, for example, lied about her age. These were minor issues. How many African American women in her time were so well traveled? Now her unnamed employer wanted to visit with Hurston. "Two more weeks and this job is over as far as I am concerned," she told her earlier, adding, "$30.00 room and board and all of the curiosity about me gives me no time to be bored."[87]

The fanfare led to her contact with Fred Koch, professor of drama at the still-segregated University of Miami. They discussed coordinating a folk festival that fall in a stadium.[88] Maybe the acclaimed ethnomusicologist Alan Lomax and Carl Sandburg, the illustrious white socialist and poet, would participate. "What do you think of it?" she asked Sandburg. "Koch was glad I suggested it, and he thinks of it as a memorial to his late, great father with whom I have worked at Chapel Hill."[89] Committed to speaking gigs, which sprang up probably as a result of the *Herald* article, she requested copies of *Seraph* from her publisher.

She next received mail at 443 East 39th, a dwelling in an industrial section of Hialeah, a growing city adjacent to Miami.[90] Cubans would often settle there following the revolution in their homeland as well as farther east in Little Havana.[91] It is uncertain who lived or worked at this address. She possibly had problems there as well, for she next took mail at a house on Northwest 63rd Street. Samuel Gomez, a newly married Bahamian, owned the home. This is the only greater Miami address where she stayed largely around people of African descent. Hurston may have met Gomez during her earlier visits to Miami or the Bahamas. His still-standing house is near Liberty Square, a public housing complex constructed in 1937 solely for African Americans.

Hurston probably saw the wall that ran a mile on West 12th Avenue between 62nd Street and 67th Street. It was built to appease white residents who did not want to live beside people of African descent, even the middle-class ones who were Liberty Square's first tenants. The development was constructed by the same WPA that had employed Hurston. Although the wall was partially demolished in the 1960s, fragments of it remain today.

Sometime in July 1950, she left for New York and returned to Florida, never to leave again. By 1951, Hurston was fixing up a rickety house in Eau Gallie, Florida, which means "water pebble." In this community, which is part of present-day Melbourne, Florida, she had written *Mules and Men*, her 1935 book of folklore she'd collected in the South. "I have a chance to buy a beautiful house on a tract of land," she told Langston Hughes while living there in 1929.[92] The price was $4,000. She just needed to put

> $1,500 down and any terms I want to make for the rest. . . . It is on the Dixie Highway, as fine a piece of road engineering as there is in the U.S.A. . . . They have never allowed a Negro to buy on the Dixie or the Indian river before and they are not doing it now, except in this case. . . . I think I can get it cheaper than 4000 if I can raise the down payment. . . . It looks absolutely safe to me, and we could have lots of fun and a lovely place to retire and write on occasion. . . . No big society stuff. Just a neat little colony of kindred souls. . . . Love and luck, honey.

Despite creating the quiet space for which she longed, Hurston also valued the company of others, including her African American peers. Even if she took political positions that irked her more progressive friends, she wanted to be among them. If she had not created the community for which she longed in Harlem, she could do it elsewhere. So she made repairs on the Eau Gallie cabin with the hope that she would finally be able to buy it and live there alone if she must.

The now-demolished house stood at the intersection of Guava Avenue and Fifth Street, now Aurora Road. It was two blocks from the Indian River, another source of comfort. There, she planted flowers that her white neighbors enjoyed stopping to see. "Somehow this one spot on earth feels like home to me," wrote Hurston to Jean Parker Waterbury, her last literary agent, adding, "I have always intended to come back here. That is why I am doing so much to make a go of it. No house in a block of me four ways. No loud radios and record-playing to irritate me, and great oaks and palms around the place."[93]

She bought a refrigerator and furniture for the house.[94] Possibly aware that she needed to take better care of her body, she also paid $67.70 on a one-year policy for health and accident insurance. But she remained frugal and asked her literary agent to set aside some of the money she earned as a freelancer. Hurston did splurge on a pair of black slacks for her visits downtown. It would cut down on the time she would spend laundering and possibly ironing a dress.[95]

As a resident of Eau Gallie, Hurston probably passed by the Libbyan, a two-story guesthouse that opened in the 1920s amid the area's initial boom.[96] It had the same Mediterranean revival style of the city hall and buildings elsewhere in the state, including Miami. She probably sent mail via the community's small brick post office.[97]

While living in Eau Gallie in 1952 and 1953, Hurston notably covered one of the most sensational trials of the 1950s as a freelance writer for the *Pittsburgh Courier*, a leading Black weekly. She was greatly interested in Ruby McCollum, a 37-year-old African American woman in Live Oak, Florida, who had killed her white lover Clifford Adams, a "poor people's" doctor and Senate hopeful who had allegedly sexually abused her.[98] The case was noteworthy because it was the first time an African American woman was permitted to testify against a white man for sexual abuse.[99] She was allowed to even say publicly that she gave birth to his child, too. Adams had also partnered with McCollum's husband in a successful numbers-running operation.[100]

An all-white jury convicted McCollum. The Supreme Court overturned the case following an appeal. Given the racial hostility surrounding her, McCollum was declared a mental incompetent and thus was unable to speak on her own behalf at a second trial. Her first-degree murder conviction and death sentence were overturned on a technicality. She was placed in an asylum until her lawyer successfully obtained her release in 1974. McCollum spent her remaining years in Silver Springs, Florida.

Hurston's commitment to covering this trial was about more than a paycheck. Even if she was a political conservative, she was aware of the injustices that people of African descent routinely faced, as McCollum's own experiences bore out. Hurston herself was unsuccessful in purchasing the Eau Gallie cabin. She apparently could not evade Jim Crow practices as she so often had.[101] The whites who liked how she fixed it and the yard up could not stand the idea of a Black woman actually owning the property.[102]

While living in Eau Gallie, Hurston also began chronicling the life of the biblical Herod but was unsuccessful in selling the book to Scribner's. By 1956, she was evicted from her cabin and relocated to Cocoa Beach, Florida, where she briefly worked as a librarian at Patrick Air Force Base before being fired. She was doubtless overqualified. As Irvine himself among others had seen, she was no idiot even as she could be strategically charming. A secure disposition was required in anyone when dealing with her.

After living in a trailer on Merritt Island, where she continued working on the book about Herod, she accepted an invitation to write a column for the *Ft. Pierce Chronicle*, a Black weekly. There, a well-to-do African American man who was aware of her legacy (and failing health) permitted her to live rent-free in a modest home that he owned. She moved to that town, where she returned to some of her earlier writings on voodoo and recast them in the column. Like Soltera and Trollope, she recycled earlier written material to stay fed. She also earned additional income as a substitute teacher.

Meanwhile, Hurston maintained a relationship with Smathers as fears of communism grew in the States. Joseph McCarthy, a US senator from Wisconsin, led the charge, often without proof, many times irking his colleagues, although

Zora Neale Hurston sits with two women, a small girl, and a dog, Ft. Pierce, Florida.
Photo B.1, Zora Neale Hurston Papers, Photographs Series B, Box 14, Folder 2, Manuscripts Collection, Special and Area Studies Collections, George A. Smathers Libraries, University of Florida, Gainesville, FL.

"the question of censuring Senator McCarthy was not and is not being dealt with," Smathers told Hurston in a 1954 letter.[103] He enclosed his additional thoughts on the matter in a letter (which he shared with Hurston) to General Sumter Lowry, a Florida National Guard commander. Within six years of receiving this personal exchange between two powerful white men, Hurston had hypertensive heart disease. After suffering a series of strokes, she died on January 28, 1960, in the St. Lucie County Welfare House. She was 69.

TAKE IT YOU'RE AMERICAN

When Hurston headed south to Honduras, she knew that she was onto something. She knew the ruins she longed to see existed. She surely knew, too, that finding them would be difficult. She went anyway. Aided by laser technology, scientists would not discover them until 2015.[1] They, not Hurston, would see the remains of the pyramids, mounds, and long plazas that had presumably sat untouched for centuries.

She searched for the ruin in the 1940s, a decade during which her country became one of the two most powerful nations in the world, alongside the Soviet Union. In a modernizing world with anxieties that included the nuclear bomb, she boldly moved. Although she did not find the ruin, she made more progress than Hugh Smythe, an African American anthropologist who was not permitted to study the Garifuna in Honduras. He began his studies at Northwestern in the 1940s with anthropologist Melville Herskovits, a scholar who traveled in the same academic circles Hurston had in New York City. Perhaps owing to fears that he might unfairly depict race relations in their country, Honduran officials denied Smythe a visa.[2] The subject of Hurston's research, the Mayans, were detached from the present, unlike the still-living Garifuna on whom Smythe concentrated.

I wish I could have walked the streets of Puerto Cortés and traveled east to the coast where the Mayan ruin sits. Given the COVID-19 pandemic and the violence down there, I could not do either. I did buy a postcard on eBay, sent on April 3, 1907, when Nicaragua was trying to overtake Honduras. In the center of the postcard is an illustration of a palm-lined road in Puerto Cortés. Around the drawing are the following words:

> We are now ashore in the American Consul's house. Ten of us under arms and ammunitions protecting the Americans from the war between Nicaragua and Honduras. We have seen a little fighting and ones of our boys was shot in the leg. This place is just like home. We expect the Nicaraguans to capture this place now anytime. Howard.[3]

The recipient of this card is a Miss Leona. If Howard safely got out of Honduras, she may have become his wife.

*

Although there are distinct differences in how their privilege as US citizen manifests, Howard and Hurston enjoyed considerable favor while in Honduras. Hers was partly borne from her fierce determination in the face of great challenge to people with dark skin. She pressed on.

During her earliest years in Harlem, she and Dorothy West tied for second place in a contest sponsored by the National Urban League's *Opportunity: A Journal of Negro Life*. West was also a core member of the Harlem Renaissance. The two women were friends, in fact. When Hurston traveled south to collect folklore, she allowed West to sublet her apartment. Because West was in her early twenties, Langston Hughes called her "the Kid."[4] And when West launched *Challenge*, her own magazine, Hurston told her:

> I love your audacity. You have learned at last the glorious lesson of living dangerously. Thats [sic] the stuff! Let the sun go down on you like King Harold at the battle of Hastings—fighting gloriously. Maybe a loser, but what a loser! Greater in defeat than the Conqueror. Certainly

not a coward that rusted out lurking in his tent—too afraid to cross your steel with fate.[5]

Because West had the audacity Hurston herself possessed, of course, she was pleased to have the youngest person in their Harlem circle solicit a submission from her. Back then, Hurston was already pushing many boundaries, including on the publishing front. She gave her an "un-Negro story" and told West if she didn't like it, she should approach *Story* magazine to see whether she could reprint her 1933 short story "The Gilded Six-Bit." Said Hurston, "The story brought me a lot of recognition" and might be suitable, especially because she did not have the time to write anything as good. She added, "Anything hurried and shoddy would hurt you as a publisher and me as a writer."[6] This letter ended, "In a big hurry darling. Yours indeed Zora."[7]

By 1948, the year that Hurston returned from Honduras (and the year she was arrested on a false charge), West saw the publication of *The Living Is Easy*, a semiautobiographical novel that recovered the experiences of the Black upper class of which she was a part. She then disappeared from the literary scene until Jackie Onassis, who was at the time a book editor, rediscovered her and offered her the opportunity to write *The Wedding*.[8]

Langston Hughes, another of Hurston's friends, also thrived, and he never lost respect for her talent. In 1953, having just finished James Baldwin's semiautobiographical *Go Tell It on the Mountain*, he decided that if "it were written by Zora Neale Hurston with her feeling for the folk idiom, it would probably be a quite wonderful book."[9] He ended the letter with this sentiment: "It ain't my meat. I wish he had collaborated with Zora."[10]

At the time, Hughes was going through papers at the Schomburg library and found some old letters from his early Harlem days. He had apparently seen some of Hurston's own letters and said, "The whole history of Zora has been unearthed!"[11] If he planned to hurt her publicly, he never followed through on this urge. Even Bontemps wrote "something from Zora perhaps" on his list of people to include in an anthology on Harlem.[12] There was no doubt of the enormity of their contributions to literature and history. As time went on, despite any misgivings about their personal relationships, her contemporaries were certain about Hurston's literary talent.

Three years after Hurston's death in 1960 and four years before his own passing, Hughes announced to Bontemps that he had come across a dusty box of old letters, some from Hurston. He was reminded of what he called "the whole Zora–MULE BONE episode."[13]

He was talking about a woman who was strategically aware of how others might see her. No one could judge her more harshly than she judged herself, though.[14] Hurston told "Godmother," her white benefactor, that compared to her brother Hezekiah, a physician and surgeon in Memphis, she was a mere "bum and Godmother's pickaninny."[15]

How much performing was required? How lonely had she been? "Never doubt that I love you and stand forever in your corner," she said via a 1957 letter to her brother Everett, who, as he had promised, left New York because of rising crime, for Cocoa, Florida. At the time, Hurston lived nearby and worked at the Patrick Air Force Base. At this point, she was ready to quit so the ones who did not "love" her could "go back to their old ways," but she would soon be fired.[16] She was close with Everett and his wife, Ivy: "I don't care a hang about anybody but you."[17] She cared for his son and namesake, too, telling him in a letter, "You don't live but once and you might as well be happy as possible on this one trip on earth."[18]

Hurston would soon gather her papers to donate to Yale University and the University of Florida. Around this time, she heard that Everett was about to purchase some land and surely he was going to plant some fruit trees. So she wrote her nephew about the most popular varieties of oranges and grapefruit: he should know about, among others, the Valencias, the Satsuma, the temple, and the king orange.[19] She had a particularly strong interest in cataloging the world around her, and her knowledge about fruit linked her to the businessmen who profited on the banana in Honduras. The distinctive way of southerners and Floridians was still on her mind as she went on to inform her nephew that "Floridians seldom eat any orange until after Christmas. We sell 'em to the Yankees before Christmas."[20] She ended this letter with, "See you later, Alligator—With all my love, Aunt Zora."[21] Aunt Zora. This is who she was to this young man. She was someone's sister, daughter, and wife.

Over the years, many US customs officials looked at her passport. Some saw the extent of her wanderlust even if they could not see the significance of her travels. In 1930, she arrived in Miami from Nassau, listing a house on 62nd Street and 19th Avenue in Liberty City as her mailing address. In 1935, she arrived again in Miami from Nassau but this time listed New York City as her home. Two years later, she arrived in New York twice from Port au Prince; the Philadelphia address for Lippincott, her then-publisher, was now where she could be reached.

As she traveled, her face was likely familiar to Edward Burke, a man who checked off the names of people entering Miami's port. On January 3, 1930, her name was typed on a manifest. Burke scratched it out and printed "Zora Hurston not on board." When Hurston showed up next in the historical record, she was in New Orleans, where she planned to study religious cults.[22] "This is where I can be found for now," Hurston seemed to be saying.

*

Other African Americans had left the States, feeling the same grief-tinged joy. Like Hurston, they were running, too. Unhappy about his encounters with racial violence in Chicago, the father of Lorraine Hansberry, the African American playwright, tried to relocate his family to Mexico prior to his death in 1946. His radical daughter, whose award-winning play *A Raisin in the Sun* was inspired by her family's travails, left the States for Mexico three years after her father's death. At the time, Hansberry took art courses at the University of Guadalajara in Ajijic.[23] Enticed by the beauty of Lake Chapala as well as the bohemian community, European, American, and Canadian expats and visitors settled in the area throughout the first half of the twentieth century.

However, neither Hansberry nor Hurston ever left this side of the Atlantic, unlike other noted African Americans, including W. E. B. Du Bois, Richard Wright, Chester Himes, and James Baldwin. Hansberry declared that "Europe never held any particular fascination for her, but the Americas did."[24] The ever-adventurous Hurston was not as dismissive. Fascinated by the "lovely letters from all over England" and continental Europe she received, she expressed a wish to do a book tour in Europe as late as 1956.[25] She never followed through. By then, her career had buckled, and she had very little money.

Years later, someone else was running. Lisa Lopes was a member of TLC, a singing group that once whispered the words "crazy . . . sexy . . . cool." Two of them were the "sexy" and the "cool." Lopes was playfully "crazy." In order to promote safe sex, she routinely drew a fat, black line under her left eye, earning the nickname "Left Eye." At the time, Lopes was also battling an alcohol addiction. Then came the first-degree arson charges in 1994, the same year her group won a Grammy. Lopes had torched a mansion in an Atlanta suburb where she lived with her NFL football player boyfriend. Fined $10,000 and sentenced to five years' probation, she sought relief from her worries in La Ceiba, a port city on Honduras's north coast. It was about 100 miles west of Puerto Cortés, where Hurston stayed in the late 1940s. There in La Ceiba, Lopes bought a condo.

She may not have known it then, but "Waterfalls," one of the big hits on her group's Grammy-winning album, was an oracle that foretold her time there. The song, which Lopes cowrote, warns listeners to avoid "moving too fast." Lopes was, indeed, moving too fast in 2002. That year, she lost control of an SUV she was driving in Honduras while trying to avoid an oncoming vehicle. She was the only one of eight people in her car who died, just before her 31st birthday. Before she passed away, she did charity work in Honduras and focused on healthy eating and spiritual practices.

*

Hurston was also deeply interested in spiritual practices but was more careless about her health, including the stomach issues that dogged her for years.[26] She once wondered whether her woes were an outcome of "impure" water she once drank in Honduras.[27] She also wondered whether her condition was connected to her earlier dabbling in voodoo. Or maybe her body was just giving out. It was yet another topic that was hard for her to discuss.

In two episodes of *She's Gotta Have It*, the 2017–2019 Netflix series inspired by Spike Lee's 1986 classic film, we glimpse the Hurston that most people love. Such people include the fictitious Nola Darling, a Black woman residing in Brooklyn who is tired of judgment, the kind that is in line with long-held thoughts about women who moan because they are just that tired.[28] In his 1727 visit to the Gold Coast, a white surveyor saw the land (they always see the land) but also saw the "hot constitution'd Ladies."[29] When she wanted, Darling could be such a lady. Maybe the three señoras could be, too, when they wanted. Darling refused such judgment. Tired women sometimes say no. Janie Mae, the protagonist in *Their Eyes,* certainly said no. She said no to two husbands and yes to the one she really wanted to be with. When we see Janie and Tea-cake and all their restless love, we see the Hurston we love. That one is easy on the ears and we celebrate her.

Darling holds flowers in honor of the Hurston who is not so complicated. The script certainly does not mention her political conservatism. Darling even smiles at the camera while declaring her regard for a woman who, not unlike herself, radically refused to be defined. By the 1940s, she wanted to say, "I found a Mayan ruin!" If only she knew that two white men found 40 of them in a single visit while traipsing through Mexico and Central America about 100 years before she got there. Still, she has much to teach us about a chase.

In days of late, I cross borders with great care. Even though I have a US passport and am a US citizen, I am cautious. A few years ago, my present husband went to Scotland to conduct research in the national library, and I joined him. We had an apartment in Leith, a funky port district a short walk from the center of Edinburgh. Our next-door neighbor, a middle-aged Scotswoman, was friendly. She happily took the hot lime, papadums, tea, cheese, and other items packed in plastic bags that we couldn't take back to the States.

This woman lived with her grandson, who was more stand-offish, but that may be because some young people can be this way. How many times did she wave at me when I left that apartment alone? How many times did I leave knowing that she was one of a few faces who would remember mine should something go wrong? The others were the white women working behind the counter of a coffee shop on the corner. A Muslim man who worked in a small grocery store, who once confused the gray scarf around my neck and the gray cloth around my head for a hijab. One day I bought a six-pack of beer. He barely held in his chuckle. He'd been duped, but he continued to smile when I repeatedly returned.

Perhaps as Hurston had whenever she left the States, I often found myself trying to find meaning in the bonds that form between human beings and the barriers that still keep us apart.

I once left a book on the dining room table. It concerned the Black Britons who in recent years have been deported to Jamaica. We were so busy with our own headlines in 2018, I'd missed this story.

My husband, a Modern British historian, saw the book.[30] Maybe I waited to hear him say the very thing he eventually said. "That photo on the cover was not taken in England," he called as if he had made some great discovery.

"Why would the photograph need to be taken in England?" I mumbled, pouring coffee into the presser. "They were sent to Jamaica. Some of them had never been to Jamaica. They know nothing about Jamaica."

"But it was not taken in England!" he repeated, already turning away.

"But why should it?" I called as he hurried away. "Why must the picture be in England?"

He did not answer. He writes checks for the important causes. He will now quietly say "San Pedro Sula" with recognition whenever he reads the latest news concerning the people who have experienced great sorrow. This is a man who has taught countless lectures about the West Indians who went to England in 1948 during a labor shortage and seem to have believed their security—security is still the thing about which I am ultimately writing with Hurston and others in Honduras and elsewhere in mind—was irrevocable, as if anything involving people who look like his wife could ever be no matter how many allies we have. One slipup and we are sent away. Fears about outsiders during the Brexit crisis led to these young Black men being sent away.

"Everywhere you'd get stopped, and it's like, why you stopping us for?" said one of them, adding, "I remember one time, I got a mate who's Albanian, and policeman come over and was like, 'You think you're black, don't you mate?' "[31]

I calmed myself and tried to remember how we are all still learning—even the ones who seem to know more about the many dangers. I am reminded now of the cranky British man who befriended my husband at the Spotted Dog pub in Neasden, a suburb of London, when he was in graduate school in the 1990s. In the common tap room, South Asians, West Indians, the Irish, and the English segregated themselves. The pub was in a neighborhood that, as Diana Evans has written in her 2006 novel about a biracial girl struggling with the devastating outcomes of her empire, "was like the high heel at the bottom of Italy. It was what the city stepped on to be sexy. London needed its Neasdens to make the Piccadilly lights, the dazzling Strand, the pigeons at Trafalgar Square and the Queen waving from her Buckingham balcony seem exciting."[32]

"I take it you're American," the man said as he followed my husband outside. "Can't say I care much for them." And yet, he weekly invited this college student from North Carolina for Sunday dinner after an incident in which he grabbed the student's hand rather than let him step toward a dicey roundabout alone. Thinking that only he could manage the dangers involved, this cranky British man said to the American, "Let me show you how to do it."

ACKNOWLEDGMENTS

I would like to thank my doctoral advisor, David Roediger, for always believing in me. My time with you as well as others at the University of Illinois Urbana–Champaign continues to inspire me.

My deep thanks to my peer reviewers for your thoughts as well as to Laura Davulis, Ezra Rodriguez, Carrie Watterson, Kristina Lykke, Kait Howard, Juliana McCarthy, Hilary Jacqmin, and so many others at or working on behalf of Johns Hopkins University Press for seeing promise in the manuscript.

I also thank the Newberry Library and Andrew W. Mellon Foundation for the time and funds to complete this book using amazing archives that even now still deepen my understanding of our historical past in Central America. My fellow spring 2021 Newberry fellows made my attempts to complete this project less lonely by surrounding me with community. Christine Adams, your friendship, ear, and sense of humor will always be remembered! Teresa Prados-Torreira, thank you for introducing me to historical actors who broaden my understanding of the hurdles that remain as we pay homage to heroes whose legacies are remembered in complicated ways. My gratitude to Newberry staffers, among them Keelin Burke, Juan Molina Hernández, and Madeline Crispell, for their assistance with the archives and other matters as I wrote this book.

Thank you, Flo Turcotte and Caleb del Rio at the University of Florida's George A. Smathers Libraries, for your assistance as I surveyed files. My gratitude goes to the staff at the Harry Ransom Center at the University of Texas at Austin for their assistance, too.

Katie Smith and Jared Johnson at the Girl Scouts of North-Central Alabama played a key role in helping me give voice to this research and the significance of reclaiming Hurston for the state of Alabama. As much as I love her ties to my home state of Florida, Hurston's beginnings in Notasulga, Alabama, make it fitting to tell her story with this state in view, too. As a former Girl Scout, I thank you for giving young girls and women a chance to know about her courage. I am also grateful for Susan Reynolds, editor at *Alabama Heritage* magazine, for seeing the possibilities and offering a chance for people residing in Alabama to learn more about Hurston's travels in and outside of the States.

Thank you to the Association for the Study of Women, Gender, and Sexuality in the South (formerly SEWSA, now WGS South) and the Association for the Study of African American Life and History (ASALH) for providing spaces where I could push my thinking on to chronicle and remember Hurston's life and work. WGS South, my gratitude to you in particular for providing a platform to share my deep interest in how African American women pursue and make claims to something that often eludes them: rest. I truly believe by the 1940s Hurston needed that and her time in Honduras was one of many ways she tried to secure it.

I truly appreciate all the people who gave me immense encouragement from the moment I announced via Twitter my signing a book contract with Johns Hopkins.

Thanks to a host of researchers and writers, still with us and now gone, among them Carla Kaplan, Virginia Moylan, Robert Hemenway, Valerie Boyd, Deborah Plant, Alice Walker, Honorée Fanonne Jeffers, Henry Louis Gates Jr., and Hazel Carby, whose published work enabled me to put together some of the puzzles involving Hurston's life. I am also grateful to numerous specialists in Latin American and Caribbean history.

There are numerous colleagues, friends, and relatives who are also owed my gratitude for their support on this project, which began as a narrative centering Black people's complex claims across time to power on the Florida peninsula. To Ken Jones, Angie Marchant, and the rest of our family in England, thank you for always being so kind and welcoming. Thank you, Sarah Fields, for your faith.

Hilary Green, a friend-sister–fellow historian, your example and excellence continue to inspire. You are among but a few souls who know many of my thoughts before I even speak. As Black women, we find hope anyway in a particular trench filled with wonder, work, and blessings. I am grateful for our scholarly and sisterly friendship. We sit and sometimes stand waiting, but always work hard for a new day.

Thank you also to Trudier Harris, my other UA Department of English colleague (O Great One!). You were there to share your thoughts about my first monograph on the complex interactions between people during the antebellum period at a history department book release event. When I took a chance and applied for the Newberry fellowship, which gave me needed time to sort through documents that would help me better understand the texture of the Honduras that existed before, during, and after Hurston's visits, you wrote one of my reference letters.

Deirdre Cooper-Owens, scholar-sister-friend, I do not know where to begin, but your gut-level thoughts, training, and foresight will always be appreciated. We are southern born and bred and know the hurdles on many fronts. We know triumphs, too. Thank you for being with me on this journey.

I am also grateful to Tiya Miles, someone I call colleague and friend. Tiya, thank you for your ear and example, too. We have separately looked at the archive via written documents but also the built environment and things that can only be held in the hand. You have found instructive meaning in the varying approaches. Thank you for starting and finishing sentences that cannot even be uttered. I see you from afar. I cheer.

Edwidge Danticat, thank you for being an exemplary way-shower with fierce vision and a sensitive heart. Inspired by you, I "create dangerously."

Leslie Casimir, it's been too long. One night not long ago in San Francisco, we whispered. We were tired, but we whispered about matters long settled and about so much that still lies ahead. Thank you, my friend, who once prepared a meal in her dorm at the University of Miami. How we have laughed there and elsewhere.

To my late colleague Howard Jones, your kind way and friendship as well as your collegiality were always deeply cherished. We read each other's work. We even talked about Central America and foreign policy together. I owe you a debt of gratitude. You remind me of what is still possible in academic life. So do you, Michael and Camille Mendle, John and Nichole Mitcham, Andrew and Zohra Lambert, Julia Brock, Cynthia and Steven Bunker, George Williamson, Larry Kohl, and Rich Megraw. Thank you also, Joshua Rothman, Kayla Key, Morta Riggs, Amy Hagedorn, and Marla Scott, for all of your help obtaining images and other matters pertaining my completion of this book.

Cleophus Thomas Jr. and Philip Hampton, I cannot thank you enough for your guidance.

Without question, I owe huge thanks to my students. Having the privilege to spend as much time with them as I do gives me faith in our future more than anything else. I stick around because of you.

To my late mentors Gloria "Gigi" Braynon Watson and "MVP," thank you for being among the ancestors. Zora, I thank you, too, for helping me to get beyond the monolithic stories. I stood on the land we call Eau Gallie and felt the wind wrap around me. I smiled, smelling, too, the Indian River you adored. I bore witness to the wonder of landscape and, above all, the Black woman's specific ability to survive if only we can carve out a bit of time to hear our own thoughts.

Thanks, my Alpha Kappa Alpha sorors Amii McKendrick, Karen Grant-Selma, Rhonda Campbell-Culver, Marie Estimé Thompson, Parrinder Stewart, Veronica Mayo, and Jennifer Campbell Preston. Thank you, my big brother, Duane Garcia Andrews (rest in peace), Jill Campbell Trent, Tonja Nunnally, Keith Braynon, Hester Bland, Nick Chiles, Cathy Pierce, Aniko Varga, Caridad de Varona, Cherise Fisher, Tina McElroy Ansa, Belay Felton, Mildred Lewis, Dawn Durante, Karen Juanita Carrillo, Arturo Otero, Dolen Perkins-Valdez, Cassander Smith, Tony Bolden, Magda Bader, Iona Andrews, and my dear mother, Estella Andrews. And finally, thank you to my colleague-mentor-friend John Beeler as well as our three feline friends for providing an ample soundtrack on the home front as I completed this book (badu badu). The beach calls us—again. The archive will join as we head out. Let's go!

NOTES

PREFACE

1. Moylan, *Zora Neale Hurston's Final Decade*.
2. Brown, " 'Dying of Cold' "; Foster-Frau and Hernández, "Freezing Temperatures and Power Outages."
3. Walker, "Light a Candle *for Raid Badawi*," 91, italics mine.
4. McKittrick, *Dear Science and Other Stories*.
5. Hemenway, *Zora Neale Hurston*; Boyd, *Wrapped in Rainbows*; Moylan, *Zora Neale Hurston's Final Decade*.
6. Stuelke, " 'Times when Greater Disciplines Are Born,' " 121.
7. Stuelke, " 'Sympathy with the Swamp.' "
8. Stuelke, " 'Sympathy with the Swamp.' "
9. She could get to it via the Patuca River. The city was in "deep jungles" of the Mosquito District—the very place she wanted to see now. In that 1930 letter, she also mentioned the Indigenous people worth studying, including the Paya, Zambu, Carib Indians, and the Mayans living on Roi Tan Island near Honduras's north coast. Hurston to Ruth Benedict, December 1930, in Kaplan, *Zora Neale Hurston*, 196.
10. Carnes, *The Failure of Union*.
11. Green, *Grant Green*. See also Sharony Green, *The Grant Green Story Part 2*, YouTube video, 20:12, October 8, 2017, at www.youtube.com/watch?v=3xs9haetVgo.
12. Wilkerson, *The Warmth of Other Suns*.
13. Andrews, "Festival for Black Author Reawakens Town to Genius," 1C.

CHAPTER ONE. AMID THE JEALOUSY AND POLITICS, SHE RUNS

1. Zora Neale Hurston to Burroughs Mitchell, January 14, 1948, in Kaplan, *Zora Neale Hurston*, 565.
2. Kaplan, *Zora Neale Hurston*, 549.
3. See drawing in Fannie Hurst collection, Harry Ransom Center, Austin, TX.

4. Hurston to Jane Belo, October 14, 1944, in Kaplan, *Zora Neale Hurston*, 510.

5. Hurston to Belo, October 14, 1944.

6. Hurston to Belo, October 14, 1944.

7. Hurston to Carl Van Vechten, "July Sunday morning, 1945," in Kaplan, *Zora Neale Hurston*, 524.

8. Van Vechten, *Nigger Heaven*.

9. James Lyons, "Famous Negro Author Working as a Maid Here Just 'to Live a Little,'" 1-B; *List of United States Citizens for Immigration Authorities*.

10. Hurston to Max Perkins, May 20, 1947, in Kaplan, *Zora Neale Hurston*, 549.

11. Hurston to Harold Spivacke, August 21, 1945, in Kaplan, *Zora Neale Hurston*, 527; For more, see Dodd, *Tiburcio Carías*.

12. Kaplan, *Zora Neale Hurston*, 25.

13. For more on Hotel Cosenza, where Hurston lodged in Puerto Cortés, from the touching perspective of a descendant of a housekeeper there, see Dell Hamilton, "Inside/Out Adventures in the Archive: Zora Neale Hurston and 'The Lost City,'" *Big Red and Shiny*, April 4, 2017, https://bigredandshiny.org/32659/insideout-adventures-in-the-archive-zora-neale-hurston-and-the-lost-city/; and Card File, Watkins-Loomis Records, Rare Book and Manuscripts, Butler Library, Columbia University.

14. *The South American Handbook*, 542.

15. Hurston to Carl Van Vechten, November 2, 1942, in Kaplan, *Zora Neale Hurston*, 466.

16. This general information and other basic statistics elsewhere in this essay are in a short report on economic activity between Honduras and the United States by the mid-twentieth century made for the American Institute of Accountants in 1947. Sources include the Consulate of Honduras in New York. See Angela Lyons, "Public Practice of Accounting in the Republic of Honduras."

17. Hurston to Maxwell Perkins, May 20, 1947, in Kaplan, *Zora Neale Hurston*, 549.

18. McKillop Wells, *Among the Garifuna*, ix.

19. Johnson, *Diaspora Conversion*, 5.

20. Euraque, "The Banana Enclave," 156.

21. Euraque, "The Banana Enclave," 156.

22. Euraque, "The Banana Enclave," 156.

23. Hurston to Max Perkins, May 20, 1947, 549.

24. Hurston to Max Perkins, May 20, 1947, 549.

25. Hurston, afterword to *Seraph on the Suwanee*, 354.

26. There are numerous sources that generally outline Honduran and Central American history, including Peckenham and Street, *Honduras*; Howard-Regundin, *Honduras*; Bethell, *Central America since Independence*.

27. Some scholars wisely do this even today. For more, see Fasquelle, "Snakes, Jaguars, and Outlaws," 1.

28. Hurston to Burroughs Mitchell, July 31, 1947, in Kaplan, *Zora Neale Hurston*, 553.

29. Hurston to Mitchell, July 31, 1947, 553.

30. Basalla, "Family Resemblances," 3; see also Mikell, "The Anthropological Imagination of Zora Neale Hurston"; Hernandez, "Multiple Subjectivities and Strategic Positionality"; Carby, "The Politics of Fiction, Anthropology and the Folk"; Gordon, "The Politics of Ethnographic Authority."

31. Basalla, "Family Resemblances," 12.

32. Basalla, "Family Resemblances," 10.

33. Banner, *Intertwined Lives*, 163.

34. Banner, *Intertwined Lives*; King, *Gods of the Upper Air*.

35. Hurston to Jane Belo, October 1, 1944, in Kaplan, *Zora Neale Hurston*, 507.

36. Hurston, *Tell My Horse*, 10.

37. *The South American Handbook*, 538.

38. The story in question is "The Admiral." The occasion for O. Henry's arrival in Honduras was his recent indictment on embezzlement charges while he was working at a Houston bank. He returned to the States for his prison sentence. Following an early release for good behavior in 1901, he wrote *Cabbages and Kings*.

39. O. Henry, *Cabbages and Kings*, 24–25.

40. Chapman, *Bananas*, 3.

41. O. Henry, *Cabbages and Kings*, 9

42. Chapman, *Bananas*, 26.

43. Chapman, *Bananas*, 26.

44. Chapman, *Bananas*, 10.

45. Chapman, *Bananas*, 24–25.

46. Chapman, *Bananas*, 30.

47. Chapman, *Bananas*, 30.

48. Chapman, *Bananas*, 11–12.

49. Chapman, *Bananas*, 24–25.

50. Chapman, *Bananas*, 36–37.

51. Chapman, *Bananas*, 36–37.

52. One Chicago company had printed more than 2.5 million photographs between 1898 and 1978. Twenty-three of the postcards featured Honduras. For more, see Curt Teich Postcard Archives Collection, Newberry Library at www.newberry.org/curt-teich-postcard-archives-collection; and Curt Teich Postcard Archives Digital Collection, Newberry Library at https://collections.carli.illinois.edu/digital/collection/nby_teich/search/searchterm/Honduras/field/state/mode/exact/conn/and/order/nosort/ad/asc/cosuppress/0.

53. The book was likely published in the 1930s, as it appears in the list of books recently received by the *Scottish Geographical Journal* in 1934. Castañeda, *Beautiful Honduras*.

54. Castañeda, *Beautiful Honduras*.

55. *The South American Handbook*, 540.

56. Fasquelle, "Snakes, Jaguars, and Outlaws," 1–2.

57. Fasquelle, "Snakes, Jaguars, and Outlaws," 4.

58. Fasquelle, "Snakes, Jaguars, and Outlaws," 4.

59. Fasquelle, "Snakes, Jaguars, and Outlaws," 4.

60. The whereabouts of photographs she apparently commissioned for travel stories about a region that increasingly intriguing to Western tourists and adventurers alike remain unknown. By the 1970s, *Holiday* merged with *Travel* magazine and subsequently sold. Hearst eventually owned the original magazine's catalog. Hurston reportedly took photographs of an eighteenth-century fort in Omoa, a small town on the north coast not far from Puerto Cortés. *Holiday* was apparently unhappy with her article and images. The latter were "too diffuse" and the former was "uninteresting." Hurston to Mitchell, July 31, 1947; Davidson, *The Lost Towns of Honduras*.

61. Hurston to Carl Van Vechten and Fania Marinoff, June 21, 1947, in Kaplan, *Zora Neale Hurston*, 550.

62. Hurston to Mitchell, July 31, 1947, 553.

63. Hurston to Mitchell, July 31, 1947, 553.

64. Hurston to Mitchell, July 31, 1947, 553.

65. Chambers, *Race, Nation and West Indian Immigration to Honduras*; McKillop Wells, *Among the Garifuna*, 67.

66. *The South American Handbook*, 385.

67. *The South American Handbook*, 385.

68. Hurston, "How It Feels to Be Colored Me," in Hurston, *I Love Myself*, 152.

69. Hurston to Spivacke, August 21, 1945, 527.

70. Max Perkins died at the front end of her stay in Central America. Hurston to Burroughs Mitchell September 3, 1947, in Kaplan, *Zora Neale Hurston*, 556.

71. Belo's husband, Frank Tannenbaum, a scholar who'd done research in Mexico, was also a recipient of this letter. Hurston to Jane Belo and Frank Tannenbaum, October 14, 1994, in Kaplan, *Zora Neale Hurston*, 511.

72. "Negro Attacked: Badly Beaten Up by Nicaraguan Soldiers," *Louisville Courier Journal*, May 4, 1907, 10.

73. Euraque, "The Banana Enclave," 151.

74. England, *Afro Central Americans*, 194; Euraque, "The Banana Enclave," 155.

75. Blumenschein, *Home in Honduras*.

76. Dodd, *Tiburcio Carías*, 9.

77. Dodd, *Tiburcio Carías*, 8.

78. John Blumenschein, a physician, died of cancer in 1958 not long after he completed their home and the clinic in Honduras.

79. Dodd, *Tiburcio Carías*, 12.

80. Dodd, *Tiburcio Carías*, 12.

81. Dodd, *Tiburcio Carías*, 12.

82. Yde, *An Archaeological Reconnaissance of Northwestern Honduras*, 27.

83. Yde, *An Archaeological Reconnaissance of Northwestern Honduras*, 27.

84. There are gaps in scholarly understanding of this issue. David J. Keeling, "Latin America's Transportation Conundrum," 133–154; and Mack, "Contraband Trade through Trujillo, Honduras," 44–56. For more, see Gauthier, "Highway Transportation and Regional Development in South America," 175–186; Brady, "Honduras' Transisthmian Corridor"; Fay and Morrison, *Infrastructure in Latin America and the Caribbean*.

85. *The South American Handbook*, 385.

86. Rey Rosa, *Dust on Her Tongue*, 29.

87. Rey Rosa, *Dust on Her Tongue*, 32.

88. Rey Rosa, *Dust on Her Tongue*, 46.

89. Rey Rosa, *Dust on Her Tongue*, 30.

90. Rey Rosa, *Dust on Her Tongue*, 52.

91. Rey Rosa, *Dust on Her Tongue*, 53.

92. Rey Rosa, *Dust on Her Tongue*, 77.

93. Rey Rosa, *Dust on Her Tongue*, 24.

94. Hurston to Franz Boas, October 20, 1929, in Kaplan, *Zora Neale Hurston*, 150–151.

95. Hurston to Burroughs Mitchell, January 14, 1948, in Kaplan, *Zora Neale Hurston*, 553.

96. Hurston to Katherine Tracy L'Engle, November 4, 1945, in Kaplan, *Zora Neale Hurston*, 535.

97. Hurston to L'Engle, November 4, 1945.

98. Lowe, *Jump at the Sun*, 21.

99. Kaplan, *Zora Neale Hurston*, 445.

100. Kaplan, *Zora Neale Hurston*, 480.

101. Arna Bontemps, "From Eatonville, Florida to Harlem," *New York Herald Tribune*, November 22, 1942, 3, quoted in Hassall, "Text and Personality in Disguise and in the Open," 159; see also Kaplan, *Zora Neale Hurston*, 436.

102. Arna Bontemps to Langston Hughes, September 8, 1942, in Nichols, *Arna Bontemps Langston Hughes Letters*, 111.

103. Bontemps to Hughes, September 8, 1942.

104. Hurston to W. E. B. Du Bois, June 11, 1945, in Kaplan, *Zora Neale Hurston*, 520.

105. Zora Neale Hurston's essay "What White Publishers Won't Print" has been reprinted in other publications, including Angelyn Mitchell, *Within the Circle: African American Literary Criticism from the Harlem Renaissance to the Present*. See also Hemenway, *Zora Neale Hurston*, 327.

106. Arna Bontemps to Langston Hughes, November 4, 1942, Nichols, *Arna Bontemps Langston Hughes Letters*, 119.

107. Kaplan, *Zora Neale Hurston*, 47.

108. Kaplan, *Zora Neale Hurston*, 47.

109. Hurston to Langston Hughes, August 17, 1929, in Kaplan, *Zora Neale Hurston*, 147.

110. Hurston to Hughes, August 17, 1929.

111. Hurston to Langston Hughes, October 15, 1929, in Kaplan, *Zora Neale Hurston*, 148.

112. Hurston to Langston Hughes, December 10, 1929, in Kaplan, *Zora Neale Hurston*, xx.

113. For more, see Kennedy, *The American People in the Great Depression*; Bindas, *Remembering the Great Depression in the Rural South*.

114. Roediger, *The Sinking Middle Class*, 30.

115. Published in 1934, Hurston's first novel, *Jonah's Gourd Vine*, centered on a Black pastor. The following year, she depicted Black folklore she had discovered in Florida in *Mules and Men*, another novel. A coming-of-age story involving a young African American woman in Florida was at the center of her best-selling 1937 novel *Their Eyes Were Watching God*. Accounts of the Afro-Caribbean rituals she studied in Haiti and Jamaica and a novel that recast the experiences of Moses can be found in *Tell My Horse: Voodoo and Life in Haiti and Jamaica* and *Moses, Man of the*

Mountain, published in 1938 and 1939, respectively. A version of her 1930 novel *Moses, Man of the Mountain* was rejected by Hollywood studios. By the late 1930s, she had been to the Caribbean several times. In 1936 and 1937, the Guggenheim Foundation funded her travel to Jamaica and Haiti. In 1942, she wrote *Dust Tracks on a Road*, a semi-autobiography. The general outlines of Hurston's life have been presented in numerous writings, among them, Hemenway, *Zora Neale Hurston*; Nathiri, *Zora Neale Hurston*; Plant, *Every Tub Must Sit on Its Own Bottom*; Wall, *Zora Neale Hurston*; Glassman and Seidel, *Zora in Florida*; Peters, *The Assertive Woman in Zora Neale Hurston's Fiction, Folklore and Drama*; Kaplan, *Zora Neale Hurston*; Bell, "Conceptualising Southern Liberalism"; Hurston and estate, *Speak So You Can Speak Again*; Boyd, *Wrapped in Rainbows*; Moylan, *Zora Neale Hurston's Final Decade*; Hurston, Gates, and West, *You Don't Know Us Negroes*.

CHAPTER TWO. FINDING A SHIP IN DAYTONA

1. Boyd, *Wrapped in Rainbows*, 369.
2. Binggeli, "The Unadapted," 6.
3. Binggeli, "The Unadapted," 6.
4. Binggeli, "The Unadapted," 6.
5. Binggeli, "The Unadapted," 6.
6. Bontemps, "From Eatonville, Florida to Harlem," 3, quoted in Hassall, "Text and Personality in Disguise and in the Open," 159; see also Kaplan, *Zora Neale Hurston*, 436.
7. The exact date of this letter, which was mailed in 1943, and the second one, which was mailed in 1939, are unknown. Bontemps wrote "Monday the 22nd" on the latter. Arna Bontemps to Langston Hughes, in Nichols, *Arna Bontemps Langston Hughes Letters*, 31 and 28.
8. Arna Bontemps to Langston Hughes, November 24, 1939, in Nichols, *Arna Bontemps Langston Hughes Letters*, 44.
9. Bontemps to Hughes, November 24, 1939.
10. Bontemps to Hughes, November 24, 1939.
11. Bontemps to Hughes, November 24, 1939.
12. Hurston to Thomas E. Jones, October 12, 1934; Hurston to Claude Burnett, December 5, 1942; and Hurston to Claude Burnett, May 16, 1943, in Kaplan, *Zora Neale Hurston*, 317, 471, 483.
13. Hurston to Thomas E. Jones, October 12, 1934, in Kaplan, *Zora Neale Hurston*, 317.
14. Hurston to Claude Barnett, May 16, 1943, in Kaplan, *Zora Neale Hurston*, 484.

15. Hurston to Barnett, May 16, 1943, 484.

16. Johnson, author of the Negro national anthem "Lift Ev'ry Voice and Sing," also wrote "You're All Right, Teddy," a campaign song for Roosevelt.

17. In 1938, Boyd also set up the Non-Partisan Council, the first group targeting issues affecting African Americans full time in Washington, DC. Before it was dissolved in 1948, the organization worked on civil rights issues with the NAACP, the Urban League, and other groups concerned with the well-being of African Americans. Boyd, one of the founders of Alpha Kappa Alpha, which became the country's first Black Greek organization in 1908, even took classes at the University of Mexico. For more, see Parker, *Past Is Prologue*, 2; McNealey, *Pearls of Service*, 49.

18. Hurston to Burnett, May 16, 1943, 483.

19. Hurston to Harold Jackman, March 29, 1944, in Kaplan, *Zora Neale Hurston*, 498.

20. Hurston to Jackman, March 29, 1944.

21. Hurston to Marjorie Kinnan Rawlings, May 16, 1943, in Kaplan, *Zora Neale Hurston*, 487. Given the invitations she was extending, Hurston apparently wanted to share the news of its ownership and the boat itself. As if reminding her acquaintances of the novelty of her achievement and the open invitation, she sometimes wrote, as in a July 23, 1943, letter to Alain Locke, "On Board Houseboat WANAGAO." Hurston to Alain Locke, July 23, 1943, in Kaplan, *Zora Neale Hurston*, 488.

22. Hurston to Jane Belo, March 20, 1940, in Kaplan, *Zora Neale Hurston*, 454.

23. Hurston to Marjorie Kinnan Rawlings, August 21, 1943, in Kaplan, *Zora Neale Hurston*, 495.

24. See State Archive, Tallahassee and clerk of courts, various counties, Tallahassee, FL, Florida, County Marriages, 1823–1982, accessed November 1, 2019, www.ancestry.com; Kaplan, *Zora Neale Hurston*, 94, 419, 570, 583, and 781.

25. Cecelski, *The Waterman's Song*; see also Bolster, *Black Jacks*.

26. Bolster, *Black Jacks*, 1. For more, see Douglass, *Narrative*; Douglass, *My Bondage and My Freedom*; Douglass, *Life and Times* (1881); Douglass, *Autobiographies*.

27. Jelly-Schapiro, *Island People*, 13.

28. Cecelski, *The Waterman's Song*.

29. Smalls would go on to serve in the South Carolina Senate and later the US House of Representatives. For larger context, see John David Smith, *Lincoln and the U.S. Colored Troops*; Luke and Smith, *Soldiering for Freedom*; John David Smith, *Black Soldiers in Blue*.

30. Cordingly, *Women Sailors and Sailors' Women*, xi–xii.

31. Cordingly, *Women Sailors and Sailors' Women*, xi–xiii.

32. Kaplan, *Zora Neale Hurston*, 541.

33. This was all wishful thinking. The vessel was destroyed and sunk in order that its owner, Timothy Meaher, a slave trader and business-man, could evade authorities. The schooner's remains were discovered in 2019. Hurston to Carita Doggett Corse, May 29, 1946, in Kaplan, *Zora Neale Hurston*, 541–542.

34. Hurston, *Barracoon*.

35. Hurston, *Barracoon*.

36. Hurston to Marjorie Kinnan Rawlings, August 21, 1943, in Kaplan, *Zora Neale Hurston*, 487.

37. Moylan, *Zora Neale Hurston's Final Decade*, 35.

38. Possibly because she knew the owner of the marina, Hurston was not policed in the manner that other Black folks in the area were sur-veilled. Mary McLeod Bethune, the founder of a historically Black col-lege in the area where Hurston had briefly taught in the mid-1930s saw her students struggle to access the city's beaches. In 1945, she purchased a small piece of land near the Indian River lagoon and the Atlantic at New Smyrna Beach, 22 miles south, for their use and the use of Black homeowners. Moylan, *Zora Neale Hurston's Final Decade*, 35; Harrison, "Once Bastion for Blacks, Bethune Beach Named Historic Site."

39. Hughes, *The Big Sea*, 239.

40. Hughes, *The Big Sea*, 239.

41. Binggeli, "The Unadapted," 8.

42. Parker with Keating, *Idella*, 87.

43. Hurston, "The Pet Negro System," repr. in Wall, *Zora Neale Hurston*, 916.

44. Hurston, "The Pet Negro System," 916.

45. She apparently traveled there to secure backing for her play *Polk County*, which she was unsuccessful in seeing produced on Broadway. Boyd, *Wrapped in Rainbows*, 377.

46. Hurston to Benjamin Botkin, July 25, 1943, in Kaplan, *Zora Neale Hurston*, 493.

47. Hurston to Harold Jackman, March 29, 1944, in Kaplan, *Zora Neale Hurston*, 498.

48. Kaplan, *Zora Neale Hurston*, 17.

49. The recipient of the letter bearing these words was Annie Nathan Meyer, a Barnard trustee and member of a prominent Jewish family. Hurston to Annie Nathan Meyer, December 13, 1925, in Kaplan, *Zora Neale Hurston*, 71.

50. Historical Currency Conversions, accessed January 3, 2021, https://futureboy.us/fsp/dollar.fsp?quantity=200&currency=dollars&fromYear=1927.

51. Hemenway, *Zora Neale Hurston*, 167.

52. Hurston to Henry Allen Moe, September 8, 1944, in Kaplan, *Zora Neale Hurston*, 501.

53. Hurston, *Tell My Horse*.

54. Hurston to Henry Allen Moe, September 18, 1944, in Kaplan, *Zora Neale Hurston*, 521–522, 504–506.

55. Hurston to Moe, September 18, 1944.

56. Kaplan, *Zora Neale Hurston*, 501.

57. My former husband, who grew up in St. Louis, recalls holding *The Latin Bit*, a 1963 album whose cover had a photograph of his father wearing a sombrero. "Bésame Mucho" and "Mambo Inn" were among the offerings. Between 1961 and 1965, his dad had made more appearances on recordings for Blue Note Records, the country's first independent jazz label. It is unsurprising that one of those albums fit the genre that was quite popular at the time. But even *Easy*, his father's final album, which was released in 1979, featured "Empanada." In fact, it is the most intriguing tune on an album that also had covers of Top 40 music like Billy Joel's 1977 hit "Just the Way You Are" and the Commodores' 1978 endearing (but in this case, plummeting) rendition of "Three Times a Lady." It is the sounds from south of the border on a tune named for a flaky Spanish pastry that make this album by a musician who will soon die of a heart attack at age 43 soar. Hurston to Harold Spivacke, August 21, 1945, in Kaplan, *Zora Neale Hurston*, 527; Green, *The Latin Bit*; Green, *Easy*.

58. Kaplan, *Zora Neale Hurston*, 501.

59. US Treasury, *Merchant Vessels of the United States, 1949*, 332.

60. US Treasury, *Merchant Vessels of the United States, 1949*, 11.

61. Hurston to Jane Belo, October 1, 1944, in Kaplan, *Zora Neale Hurston*, 507.

62. Hurston to Belo, October 1, 1944.

63. Hurston to Belo, October 1, 1944.

64. Hurston to Belo, October 1, 1944.

65. Hurston to Carl Van Vechten, July 24, 1945, in Kaplan, *Zora Neale Hurston*, 525.

66. Hurston to Jane Belo and Frank Tannenbaum, October 14, 1944, in Kaplan, *Zora Neale Hurston*, 510.

67. Hurston to Belo and Tannenbaum, October 14, 1944, 510.

68. Hurston to Belo and Tannenbaum, October 14, 1944, 511.

69. Hurston to Belo and Tannenbaum, October 14, 1944, 511.

70. Hurston to Belo and Tannenbaum, October 14, 1944, 511.

71. Hurston to Jane Belo and Frank Tannenbaum, October 18, 1944, in Kaplan, *Zora Neale Hurston*, 512.

72. Hurston to Belo and Tannenbaum, October 18, 1944, 511, 513.

73. Hurston to Henry Allen Moe, October 18, 1944, in Kaplan, *Zora Neale Hurston*, 514.

74. Hurston to Claude Barnett, April 28, 1945, in Kaplan, *Zora Neale Hurston*, 517.

75. Hurston to W. E. B. Du Bois, June 11, 1945, in Kaplan, *Zora Neale Hurston*, 518.

76. Hurston to Du Bois, June 11, 1945, 518.

77. Hurston to Du Bois, June 11, 1945, 518.

78. Hurston to Du Bois, June 11, 1945, 519.

79. Jennings, *Through the Shadows with O. Henry.*

80. Jennings, *Through the Shadows with O. Henry.*

81. Jennings, *Through the Shadows with O. Henry*, 76.

82. Jennings, *Through the Shadows with O. Henry*, 78.

83. Getz and Gilberto, "The Girl from Ipanema."

84. Getz and Gilberto, "The Girl from Ipanema."

85. Hurston to Burroughs Mitchell, September 3, 1947, in Kaplan, *Zora Neale Hurston*, 556.

86. Chapman, *Bananas*, 20.

87. Chapman, *Bananas*, 48.

88. Chapman, *Bananas*, 41.

89. For more, see Cohen, *The Fish That Ate the Whale*; Davidson, *Etnologia y etnohistoria de Honduras.*

90. Chapman, *Bananas*, 61.

91. Chapman, *Bananas*, 3; Colby, *The Business of Empire.*

92. Putnam, *Radical Moves*, 27.

93. Putnam, *Radical Moves*, 68.

94. Yde, *An Archaeological Reconnaissance of Northwestern Honduras.*

95. Andrews, *Research and Reflections.*

96. Kaplan, *Zora Neale Hurston*, 836.

97. His plantation was in Costa Rica.

98. Kaplan, *Zora Neale Hurston*, 836.

99. Chapman, *Bananas*, 19.

100. Chapman, *Bananas*, 13. The banana trivia in this section is largely from Chapman's *Bananas*.

101. *Working Girl*, dir. Nichols; *The Bird Cage*, dir. Nichols.

102. *Girls Trip*, dir. Lee.

103. Chapman, *Bananas*, 21.

104. Carby, *Imperial Intimacies*, 29.

105. Carby, *Imperial Intimacies*, 32.

106. Carby, *Imperial Intimacies*, 3.

107. Campt, *Listening to Images*, 43.

108. Campt, *Listening to Images*, 45.

109. Selvon, *The Lonely Londoners*.

110. Selvon, *The Lonely Londoners*, 31.

111. *Appointment in Honduras*, dir. Tourneur. See also Fujiwara, *The Cinema of Nightfall*, 209–217.

112. *Bananas*, dir. Allen.

113. Chapman, *Bananas*.

114. Chapman, *Bananas*, 77.

115. Chapman, *Bananas*, 79.

116. Putnam, *Radical Moves*, 98.

117. Putnam, *Radical Moves*, 80.

118. Putnam, *Radical Moves*, 80.

119. Benjamin, *Don't Be Afraid, Gringo*, 18.

120. Benjamin, *Don't Be Afraid, Gringo*, 1.

121. Benjamin, *Don't Be Afraid, Gringo*, 88.

122. Benjamin, *Don't Be Afraid, Gringo*, 110, 112.

123. Benjamin, *Don't Be Afraid, Gringo*, 27.

124. Chapman, *Bananas*, 3.

125. The statistics in this section are largely from Alvarado's book. For context, see LaFeber, *Inevitable Revolutions*, and Euraque, *Reinterpreting the Region and State in the Banana Republic*, among other sources.

CHAPTER THREE. SEEING "DIFFUSED PINKNESS"

1. Hurston, *Seraph on the Suwanee*.

2. Hurston, *Dust Tracks on the Road*, 233–234.

3. R. J. Smith, *The Great Black Way*, 49.

4. R. J. Smith, *The Great Black Way*, 43–45.

5. R. J. Smith, *The Great Black Way*, 40.

6. R. J. Smith, *The Great Black Way*, 33.

7. R. J. Smith, *The Great Black Way*, 54.

8. Binggeli, "The Unadapted," 3.

9. Thurman, *Infants of the Spring*; Wintz, *Remember the Harlem Renaissance*, 158.

10. Hurston, *Seraph*, x.

11. Thurman, *Infants of the Spring*, 10.

12. Langston Hughes to Arna Bontemps, May 26, 1941, in Nichols, *Arna Bontemps Langston Hughes Letters*, 82.

13. Hughes to Bontemps, May 26, 1941, 82.

14. R. J. Smith, *The Great Black Way*, 23.

15. Langston Hughes to Arna Bontemps, September 28, 1941, in Nichols, *Arna Bontemps Langston Hughes Letters*, 89.

16. Hughes to Bontemps, September 28, 1941, 89.

17. Hughes to Bontemps, September 28, 1941, 89.

18. Hughes to Bontemps, September 28, 1941, 89.

19. Hurston to Katherine Tracy L'Engle, February 19, 1946, in Kaplan, *Zora Neale Hurston*, 539.

20. Hemenway, *Zora Neale Hurston*, 310.

21. Boyd, *Wrapped in Rainbows*, 395.

22. Charles, "Talk about the South."

23. In a September 1947 letter, Hurston told her editor, "I am posting the second part of the book today." Hurston to Burroughs Mitchell, September 3, 1947, in Kaplan, *Zora Neale Hurston*, 554.

24. Hurston, *Seraph on the Suwanee*, 326.

25. Charles, "Talk about the South," 19.

26. Hurston to Mitchell, October 2, 1947, 558.

27. Hurston to Mitchell, October 2, 1947, 558.

28. Kaplan, *Zora Neale Hurston*, 558–559.

29. Hurston, *Seraph on the Suwanee*, 105–124, 323. Numerous writings address the plot and characters in Hurston's *Seraph*, among them, Rieger, "Working-Class Pastoral"; Lowe, *Jump at the Sun*; St. Clair, "The Courageous Undertow of Zora's *Seraph on the Suwanee*"; Tate, "Hitting 'A Straight Lick with a Crooked Stick'"; Dubeck, "The Social Geography of Race"; Jackson, "Waste and Whiteness."

30. Hurston, *Seraph on the Suwanee*, 323.

31. Hurston, *Seraph on the Suwanee*, ix.

32. Hurston to Mitchell, October 2, 1947, 559.

33. Boyd, *Wrapped in Rainbows*, 392.

34. Zora Neale Hurston to Franz Boaz, October 20, 1920, in Kaplan, *Zora Neale Hurston*, 150.

35. Guterl, *American Mediterranean*.

36. Jelly-Schapiro, *Island People*, 12.

37. In 2021, Colombia allowed temporary legal status to undocumented migrants from Venezuelans fleeing economic instability in their homeland under an authoritarian regime. This move poses tensions with the country's formal acknowledgment of Indigenous people and people of African descent late in the past century because in both cases, the

Colombian government appears to be open to politically helping ostracized communities. This is the case even if pertinent distinctions exist between Native people and people of African descent in Colombia and among Venezuelan migrants. Otis, "Colombia's President on Amnesty for Venezuelans"; Helg, *Liberty and Equality in Caribbean Colombia.* Understanding Blackness, depending on whether one is inside or outside of the Caribbean, is also critical to seeing how some strategic maneuvers in oppressed populations manifest. For more, see Brock and Fuertes, *Between Race and Empire*; and Carby, *Imperial Intimacies.*

38. For more, see Anderson, *Black and Indigenous*; MacRae Taylor, *The Black Carib of British Honduras*; Chomsky and Lauria-Santiago, *Identity and Struggle at the Margins of the Nation-State*; England, *Afro Central Americans*; Johnson, *Diaspora Conversion*; Anderson, *Black and Indigenous*; Euraque and Martinez, *The African Diaspora in the Educational Programs of Central America*; de la Fuente and Andrews, *Estudios Afrolatinoamericanos*; Gudmundson and Wolfe, *Blacks and Blackness in Central America*; Sierakowski, "Central America's Caribbean Coast"; Putnam, *Radical Moves*; Chambers, *Race, Nation and West Indian Immigration to Honduras.*

39. Hurston, *Seraph on the Suwanee*, 327.

40. Hurston, Seraph on the Suwanee, 326.

41. Hurston, *Seraph on the Suwanee*, 327.

42. Hurston, *Seraph on the Suwanee*, 327.

43. Hurston, *Seraph on the Suwanee*, 328.

44. Hurston, *Seraph on the Suwanee*, 328.

45. Hurston, *Seraph on the Suwanee*, 323.

46. Hurston, *Seraph on the Suwanee*, 328.

47. Hurston, *Seraph on the Suwanee*, 329.

48. Hurston, *Seraph on the Suwanee*, 330.

49. Hurston, *Seraph on the Suwanee*, 330.

50. Hurston, *Seraph on the Suwanee*, 333.

51. Hurston, *Seraph on the Suwanee*, 335.

52. Hurston, *Seraph on the Suwanee*, 335–336.

53. Hurston, *Seraph on the Suwanee*, 337.

54. Hurston, *Seraph on the Suwanee*, 339.

55. Hurston, *Seraph on the Suwanee*, 339.

56. Hurston, *Seraph on the Suwanee*, 342.

57. Hurston, *Seraph on the Suwanee*, 14.

58. Charles, "Talk about the South," 20.

59. Charles, "Talk about the South," 4.

60. Binggeli, "The Unadapted," 4.

61. Charles, "Talk about the South," 7.

62. Carby, in Hurston, *Seraph on the Suwanee*, xiv.

63. Hurston to Burroughs Mitchell, September 3, 1947, in Kaplan, *Zora Neale Hurston*, 555.

64. Hurston to Mitchell, September 3, 1947, 555.

65. Hurston to Mitchell, September 3, 1947, 555.

66. Hurston to Mitchell, September 3, 1947, 555.

67. Wells, *Explorations and Adventures*, 119.

68. *Incidents of Travel*.

69. For more on the origins and decline of Mayan civilization, see Brunhouse, *In Search of the Maya*; Culbert, *The Lost Civilization*; Lange, "Central America and the Southwest," 140; Alonzo, *An Overview of the Mayan World*; Coe, *The Maya*; Nations, *The Maya Tropical Forest*.

70. Lange, "Central America and the Southwest," 160.

71. Lange, "Central America and the Southwest," 162.

72. John Potts to Henry Cook, June 28, 1829, "Copies of letters and accounts from 1821–1831 concerning efforts by John Potts Esq. to seek compensation for himself and his sisters for Indian slaves freed in the British settlement of Honduras," Edward E. Ayer Manuscript Collection, Newberry Library.

73. *The Mosquito Coast*, dir. Weir; *The Mosquito Coast*, dir. Wyatt.

74. Young, *Narrative of a Residence on the Mosquito Shore*, 13.

75. Young, *Narrative of a Residence on the Mosquito Shore*, 16.

76. Young, *Narrative of a Residence on the Mosquito Shore*, 28.

77. Young, *Narrative of a Residence on the Mosquito Shore*, 24.

78. Young, *Narrative of a Residence on the Mosquito Shore*, 29; Jolly, *Jackspeak*.

79. Young, *Narrative of a Residence on the Mosquito Shore*, 107.

80. He was, however, generous in praising the women in the Sambo Indigenous community, who "when young, and before hard labour and precarious living alter them, are frequently handsome and well proportioned." Young, *Narrative of a Residence on the Mosquito Shore*, 75, 123.

81. Young, *Narrative of a Residence on the Mosquito Shore*, 75.

82. Young, *Narrative of a Residence on the Mosquito Shore*, 141.

83. Young, *Narrative of a Residence on the Mosquito Shore*, 141–142.

84. Wells, *Explorations and Adventures*, xi.

85. Wells, *Explorations and Adventures*, xiii.

86. Wells, *Explorations and Adventures*, xv.

87. Wells, *Explorations and Adventures*, 119.

88. Wells, *Explorations and* Adventures, 122.

89. Wells, *Explorations and Adventures*, 122.

90. Wells, *Explorations and Adventures*, 124.

91. Wells, *Explorations and Adventures*, 128.

92. Wells, *Explorations and Adventures*, 128.

93. For more on some of the earliest scholarly visits to Central America, see Beaudry-Corbett and Hardy, *Early Scholars' Visits to Central America*.

94. The information presented in this paragraph is based on the land use recorded on a 1983 map. It is highly likely Hurston encountered land conditions that were somewhat similar. The exact conditions under which traveled may be gained during ongoing research. Map courtesy of Perry Castañeda Map Collection, University of Texas at Austin.

95. Hemenway, *Zora Neale Hurston*, 222.

96. Hurston, *Their Eyes Were Watching God*, 24.

97. Fasquelle, "Snakes, Jaguars, and Outlaws," 4.

98. Fasquelle, "Snakes, Jaguars, and Outlaws," 5.

99. Fasquelle, "Snakes, Jaguars, and Outlaws," 5.

100. Fasquelle, "Snakes, Jaguars, and Outlaws," 5.

101. Blumenschein, *Home in Honduras*, 35.

102. Blumenschein, *Home in Honduras*, 34.

103. Blumenschein, *Home in Honduras*, 37.

104. Blumenschein, *Home in Honduras*, 5–6.

105. Blumenschein, *Home in Honduras*, 7.

CHAPTER FOUR. THE TWO WHO WERE DUPED BUT RESISTED EXPECTATION

1. María Soltera is the pen name for an English woman named Mary Lester. The legendary archaeologist Doris Stone, a pioneer woman researcher in Central America, edited the 1964 account of Soltera's trip. As earlier mentioned, Stone was the daughter of Samuel Zemurray, the Russian immigrant who oversaw the United Fruit Company. Sears, *John Neal*, 99. For more, see Pattee, preface to *American Writers*; Finkelstein, *The House of Blackwood*; Finklestein, *Print Culture and the Blackwood Tradition*; Soltera, *A Lady's Ride*; Lara, "Gendered National Bodies & Racial Difference in *A Lady's Ride*."

2. Soltera, *A Lady's Ride*, 308.

3. Soltera, *A Lady's Ride*, xx–xxii.

4. There are numerous biographical writings on Burton, including Lovell, *A Rage to Live*.

5. Floyd, *The Anglo-Spanish Struggle for Mosquitia*; Naylor, *Penny Ante Imperialism*.

6. Lara, "Gendered National Bodies & Racial Difference in *A Lady's Ride*," 206.

7. Soltera, *A Lady's Ride*, 8.

8. Hurston to Lawrence Jordan, March 24, 1927, in Kaplan, *Zora Neale Hurston*, 95.

9. Hurston to Jordan, March 24, 1927, 95.

10. Hurston to Langston Hughes, postmarked September 5, 1929, in Kaplan, *Zora Neale Hurston*, 148.

11. Hurston to Hughes, September 5, 1929, 148.

12. Soltera, *A Lady's Ride*, xii; LaFeber, *Inevitable Revolutions*; Euraque, *Reinterpreting the Region*; Peckenham and Street, *Honduras*.

13. A Mary Lester appears on the manifest of a ship leaving Honduras at the approximate time Soltera said she left the country. The woman's approximate date of birth is the same as a Mary Lester whose father was a twice-married bartender in England. His daughter Mary once lived in a workhouse, an institution for people who labored in exchange for housing and meals. Unless she acquired money in some unknown fashion that enabled her trip overseas, it is unlikely that woman is Soltera. She certainly appears to have been fluent in both Spanish and French. Linguistic skills enabling such proficiency probably would not have been acquired in a workhouse. That said, the well-traveled Englishman Charles Dickens worked in a factory after his father was placed in a debtor's prison. New Orleans, Passenger Lists, 1813–1963 for Mary Lester; 1861 England Census, accessed March 1, 2021, www.ancestry.com. For more, see, among many publications, Schlicke, *The Oxford Companion to Charles Dickens*; Ledger and Furneaux, *Charles Dickens in Context*; Soltera, *A Lady's Ride*, x and 52.

14. Hurston to Henry Allen Moe, October 18, 1944, in Kaplan, *Zora Neale Hurston*, 514.

15. Soltera, *A Lady's Ride*, 5.

16. For more, see, among others, Pratt, *Imperial Eyes and Transculturation*; Mills, *Discourses of Difference*; Mercer, "Gender and Genre in Nineteenth Century Travel Writing"; Bohls, *Women Travel Writers*; Bassnett, "Travel Writing and Gender"; Thompson, *Travel Writing*; Wagner, "Travel Writing."

17. Lambert, *Crusoe's Island*.

18. Trollope, *Domestic Manners of the Americans*, 7, emphasis added. See also Green, *Remember Me to Miss Louisa*, 121.

19. Potter, *A Hairdresser's Experience in High Life*.

20. Horton and Flaherty, "Black Leadership in Antebellum Cincinnati," 81. For more, see Green, *Remember Me to Miss Louisa*.

21. Green, *Remember Me to Miss Louisa*, 28; Potter, *A Hairdresser's Experience*.

22. Green, *Remember Me to Miss Louisa*, 281. For more, see Mattison and Picquet, *The Octoroon*.

23. Soltera, *A Lady's Ride*, 55.

24. Soltera, *A Lady's Ride*, 73.

25. Soltera, *A Lady's Ride*, 77.

26. Soltera, *A Lady's Ride*, 80.

27. Soltera, *A Lady's Ride*, 107–108.

28. Soltera, *A Lady's Ride*, 77.

29. I was unable to establish the veracity of Soltera's account of her father's military service.

30. Foner, *Antonio Maceo*, 7–9.

31. Soltera, *A Lady's Ride*, 10.

32. Soltera, *A Lady's Ride*, 1, 3.

33. Soltera, *A Lady's Ride*, 3–4.

34. Maceo's experiences reveal the possibilities for people in the African diaspora when they acknowledge one another, as well as the possibilities when anyone *acts* on the distress facing any historically oppressed group. The promises in either case are displayed in *The Mali-Cuba Connection*, a film paying tribute to ten young musicians from Mali whom Fidel Castro allowed to study music in Cuba during the 1960s. Social revolutions in various countries were in the backdrop of his invitation. The times were so horrific, Bocana Maïga, one of the Malian musicians who studied in Cuba, left his homeland for Côte d'Ivoire. He later returned to Cuba to perform with the people who had earlier welcomed him and his fellow Malians. I first saw *The Mali-Cuba Connection*, also called *Africa Mia*, when it was among the motion pictures presented at the Ninth Annual Tuscaloosa Africana Film Festival. For more, see *The Mali-Cuba Connection*, dir. Minier.

35. Soltera, *A Lady's Ride*, 2.

36. Soltera, *A Lady's Ride*, 108.

37. Soltera, *A Lady's Ride*, 24.

38. Soltera, *A Lady's Ride*, 108–111.

39. Soltera, *A Lady's Ride*, 75.

40. Soltera, *A Lady's Ride*, 58.

41. Soltera, *A Lady's Ride*, 65 and 69.

42. Soltera, *A Lady's Ride*, 70–71.

43. Soltera, *A Lady's Ride*, 96.

44. Soltera, *A Lady's Ride*, 93 and 109.

45. Soltera, *A Lady's Ride*, 96.

46. Soltera, *A Lady's Ride*, 100.
47. Soltera, *A Lady's Ride*, 118.
48. Soltera, *A Lady's Ride*, 123.
49. Soltera, *A Lady's Ride*, 80.
50. Soltera, *A Lady's Ride*, 132.
51. Soltera, *A Lady's Ride*, 127.
52. Soltera, *A Lady's Ride*, 138.
53. Soltera, *A Lady's Ride*, 162–163.
54. Soltera, *A Lady's Ride*, 149 and 115.
55. Soltera, *A Lady's Ride*, 156.
56. Soltera, *A Lady's Ride*, 156.
57. Soltera, *A Lady's Ride*, 160.
58. Soltera, *A Lady's Ride*, xiv.
59. Soltera, *A Lady's Ride*, 165.
60. Soltera, *A Lady's Ride*, 168.
61. Soltera, *A Lady's Ride*, 169.
62. Soltera, *A Lady's Ride*, 172–173.
63. Soltera, *A Lady's Ride*, 174.
64. Soltera, *A Lady's Ride*, 176–177.
65. Soltera, *A Lady's Ride*, 178–179.
66. Soltera, *A Lady's Ride*, 179–180.
67. Soltera, *A Lady's Ride*, 180–181.
68. Soltera, *A Lady's Ride*, 184–185.
69. Soltera, *A Lady's Ride*, 187–189.
70. Soltera, *A Lady's Ride*, 191.
71. Soltera, *A Lady's Ride*, 193.
72. Soltera, *A Lady's Ride*, 203.
73. Soltera, *A Lady's Ride*, 207.
74. Soltera, *A Lady's Ride*, 209–211.
75. Soltera, *A Lady's Ride*, 214.
76. Soltera, *A Lady's Ride*, 227.
77. Soltera, *A Lady's Ride*, 231.
78. Soltera, *A Lady's Ride*, 241.
79. Soltera, *A Lady's Ride*, 249.
80. Soltera, *A Lady's Ride*, 250–251.
81. Soltera, *A Lady's Ride*, 256.
82. Soltera, *A Lady's Ride*, 263.
83. Soltera, *A Lady's Ride*, 263.
84. Soltera, *A Lady's Ride*, 272.
85. Soltera, *A Lady's Ride*, 283.
86. Soltera, *A Lady's Ride*, 312.

87. Soltera, *A Lady's Ride*, 312.

88. Soltera, *A Lady's Ride*, 309–310.

89. Soltera, *A Lady's Ride*, 309–310.

90. Lara, "Gendered National Bodies & Racial Difference in *A Lady's Ride*," 209.

91. Lara, "Gendered National Bodies & Racial Difference in *A Lady's Ride*," 210.

92. She, for example, helped Thomas Campbell-Copeland prepare a reference book about Cuba, Puerto Rico, the Philippines, Guam, and Hawaii. Soltera, *A Lady's Ride*, x; Campbell-Copeland and Soltera, *American Colonial Handbook*.

93. Hurston to Burroughs Mitchell, February 14, 1948, in Kaplan, *Zora Neale Hurston*, 569.

94. Hurston to Burroughs Mitchell, December 5, 1947, in Kaplan, *Zora Neale Hurston*, 564.

95. Hurston to Burroughs Mitchell, January 14, 1948, in Kaplan, *Zora Neale Hurston*, 565.

96. Egon Mathiesen, a Dutch children's picture book illustrator, sent one of the two final letters that Hurston received in Honduras. She and Mathiesen were apparently exchanging books, as she promised to send him a copy of *Mules and Men*, her 1935 book. Hurston to Egon Mathiesen, January 22, 1948, in Kaplan, *Zora Neale Hurston*, 566–567.

97. Euraque, *Reinterpreting the Region* 11.

98. Romney, *Land in British Honduras*, 1.

99. Romney, *Land in British Honduras*, 2.

100. Romney, *Land in British Honduras*, 2.

101. Dodd, *Tiburcio Carías*, 1356.

102. Arthur Thrupp to Peter Cracroft, September 11, 1863, enclosed in Alexander Milne to the Secretary of the Admiralty, British National Archives, ADM1/5821.

103. Thrupp to Cracroft, September 18, 1863, enclosed in Alexander Milne to the Secretary of the Admiralty.

104. Hurston to Mitchell, February 14, 1948, 568–569.

CHAPTER FIVE. HEALING IN MIAMI BEFORE A FAILED RETURN

1. Hurston to Carl Van Vechten and Fania Marinoff, October 30, 1948, in Kaplan, *Zora Neale Hurston*, 573.

2. Boyd, *Wrapped in Rainbows*, 388.

3. Hurston to Van Vechten and Marinoff, October 30, 1948; Hurston to Helen Worden Erskine, February 4, 1949; Hurston to Fannie Hurst, February 10, 1949; Hurston to Helen Worden Erskine, May 2, 1949, in Kaplan, *Zora Neale Hurston*, 570–574, 578–580, 582–584. See also Boyd, *Wrapped in Rainbows*, 398.

4. Hemenway, *Zora Neale Hurston*, 309.

5. Hemenway, *Zora Neale Hurston*, 322.

6. Hurston to Fannie Hurst, fall/winter 1948, in Kaplan, Zora Neale Hurston, 574

7. Hurston to Van Vechten and Marinoff, October 30, 1948, 572.

8. What happened to the *Maridome*, the ship he planned to use earlier, is another thing that is unclear.

9. She sold a short story to the *Saturday Evening Post*.

10. Hurston to Burroughs Mitchell. The exact date is unclear. She wrote only "Winter 1950." In Kaplan, *Zora Neale Hurston*, 623.

11. Hurston to Max Perkins, May 20, 1947, in Kaplan, *Zora Neale Hurston*, 549.

12. Morgan, *Laboring Women*, 44–45.

13. Hurston to Mitchell, "Winter 1950," 621.

14. Hurston to Mitchell, "Winter 1950," 621.

15. Hurston to Mitchell, "Winter 1950," 623.

16. Hurston to Mitchell, "Winter 1950," 622.

17. Hurston to Mitchell, "Winter 1950," 623.

18. Hemenway, *Zora Neale Hurston*; Boyd, *Wrapped in Rainbows*, 377.

19. Dunn, *Black Miami in the Twentieth Century*, 58.

20. Fisher, Fabulous Hoosier, 85.

21. The history of Miami Beach is offered in numerous writings including Federal Writers' Project, *Florida*.

22. Federal Writers' Project, *Florida*, 84.

23. Boyd, *Wrapped in Rainbows*, 407.

24. This data comes from a report published in 1951 that was prepared by Victor W. Bennett and Barton A. Westerlund, two University of Miami instructors. See *A Survey of the Winter Tourist Industry of Greater Miami*, 20.

25. Bennett and Westerlund, *A Survey of the Winter Tourist Industry of Greater Miami*, 3.

26. Bennett and Westerlund, *A Survey of the Winter Tourist Industry of Greater Miami*, 11.

27. Mohl, Graff, and Zoloth, *South of the South*, 38.

28. Mohl, Graff, and Zoloth, *South of the South*, 38.

29. Most of the plot development in the 2020 Regina King film *One Night in Miami* takes place in a facsimile of this hotel. There, NFL player Jim Brown, singer Sam Cooke, activist Malcolm X, and a boxer, then named Cassius Clay, discuss weighty matters concerning race relations. "Fla's Hampton House Offers Fun under the Sun," *New York Amsterdam News*, December 16, 1961, 31; "Hampton House, Plush Miami Center, Now Open," *Atlanta Daily World*, November 8, 1961, 5; Emmrich, "Has the Oscars Race Already Narrowed?"

30. For more, see Lipsytes, "Clay Discusses His Future," 34.

31. Hurston to Mitchell, "Winter 1950," 623.

32. Dickinson, "Florida's Senatorial Slugfest was Bitter, Ugly, Legendary."

33. Clark, *Red Pepper and Gorgeous George*, 133.

34. Clark, *Red Pepper and Gorgeous George*, 131.

35. Clark, *Red Pepper and Gorgeous George*, 132.

36. Clark, *Red Pepper and Gorgeous George*, 167.

37. Hofstadter, "The Paranoid Style in American Politics."

38. Hurston to Benjamin Botkin, October 6, 1944, in Kaplan, *Zora Neale Hurston*, 509.

39. Kaplan, *Zora Neale Hurston*, 629.

40. Akhtar, *Homeland Elegies.*

41. Akhtar, *Homeland Elegies*, 15.

42. Akhtar, *Homeland Elegies*, 15.

43. Akhtar, *Homeland Elegies*, 17.

44. Akhtar, *Homeland Elegies*, 24.

45. Akhtar, *Homeland Elegies*, 24.

46. Hurston to Burroughs Mitchell, February 3, 1950, in Kaplan, *Zora Neale Hurston*, 763.

47. Hurston to Mitchell, February 3, 1950, 763.

48. Hurston to Mary Holland, October 21, 1958, in Kaplan, *Zora Neale Hurston*, 771.

49. Bell, "Conceptualising Southern Liberalism," 38.

50. R. G. Danner to county chairman, April 3, 1950, Political—1950 Campaign—Bulletins and Press Releases, George Smathers Papers.

51. R. G. Danner to county chairman, March 6, 1950, Political—1950 Campaign—Bulletins and Press Releases, George Smathers Papers.

52. R. G. Danner to county chairman, March 3, 1950, Political—1950 Campaign—Bulletins and Press Releases, George Smathers Papers.

53. R. G. Danner to county chairman, March 3, 1950.

54. Hurston, "I Saw Negro Votes Peddled."

55. Hurston, "I Saw Negro Votes Peddled."

56. Clark, *Red Pepper and Gorgeous George*, 113.

57. Nina Simone, "My Sweet Lord / Today Is a Killer." I am especially attuned to the way Simone improvised these words. They came from somewhere deep inside of her and emerge as part of a little-seen and little-discussed archive, the sort that is not easily named but remains real. Its source has diasporic resonances and is a response to senseless death like the sort seen during the Vietnam War and elsewhere. For more, see McKittrick, *Dear Science and Other Stories*.

58. Jones, *My Lai*, 1–2.

59. Jones, *My Lai*, 3.

60. Jones, *My Lai*, 50.

61. See Stuckey, *Slave Culture*; and Canter Brown Jr., *Florida's Black Public Officials*, 5.

62. Richardson, *African Americans in the Reconstruction of Florida*, 16.

63. Canter Brown Jr., *Florida's Black Public Officials*, 15.

64. Canter Brown Jr., *Florida's Black Public Officials*, 16.

65. *Writer's Program of the Works Progress Administration in the State of Florida, Guide to Key West*, 24.

66. Ogle, *Key West*, 6.

67. Beeler, *Milne Papers*, 2:211.

68. Gonzalez-Tennant, *The Rosewood Massacre*; McGovern, *Anatomy of a Lynching*; Wilkerson, *The Warmth of Other Suns*, 58–62. For more, see Hollar, *Thirteen Loops*.

69. Numerous writers have addressed Hurston's research on Florida's turpentine industry. Select works including Nicholls, "Migrant Labor, Folklore, and Resistance"; Mormino, "Florida Slave Narratives"; Porter, "Editor's Introduction."

70. Milne to David Milne, November 1838, in Beeler, *Milne Papers*, 1:82.

71. Beeler, *Milne Papers*, 1:82.

72. Beeler, *Milne Papers*, 1:54.

73. Beeler, *Milne Papers*, 1:54. See also Zoloth, "Miami Integration"; Diner, Kohn, and Kranson, *A Jewish Feminine Mystique?*

74. Frank Smathers to Zora Neale Hurston, undated, Box 2, Folder 86, Zora Neale Hurston Papers, George A. Smathers Special and Area Collections, University of Florida Libraries.

75. Smathers to Hurston, undated.

76. Lura Smathers to Zora Neale Hurston, undated, Zora Neale Hurston Papers, Box 2, Folder 87, Special and Area Collections, George A. Smathers Libraries, University of Florida; Crispell, *Testing the Limits*, 2.

77. Kaplan, *Zora Neale Hurston*, 559.

78. She scribbled "115 First Terrace" on a letter, but the house was almost certainly at 115 First Rivo Alto Terrace, as there was no First Terrace.

79. *Miami Herald*, March 26, 1950; *Miami Herald*, March 1, 1950, 2-A.

80. Volte, "Private Negro Housing Plan Called Hodge-Podge."

81. Mohl, "'South of the South?,'" 22.

82. Mohl, "'South of the South?,'" 22.

83. Mohl, "'South of the South?,'" 22.

84. Mohl, "'South of the South?,'" 22.

85. Mohl, "'South of the South?,'" 22.

86. Mohl, "'South of the South?,'" 22.

87. Mohl, "'South of the South?,'" 22.

88. "Frederick Koch, 88."

89. Hurston to Carl Sandburg, June 12, 1950, in Kaplan, *Zora Neale Hurston*, 628.

90. While she wrote "NE 49th" Street in her correspondence, it is more likely that the correct address was East 49th Street in Hialeah.

91. Kaplan, *Zora Neale Hurston*, 627.

92. Hurston to Langston Hughes, May 31, 1929, in Kaplan, *Zora Neale Hurston*, 145.

93. Hurston to Jean Parker Waterbury, July 9, 1951, in Kaplan, *Zora Neale Hurston*, 663.

94. Raley and Raley, *Melbourne and Eau Gallie*, 74.

95. Hurston to Waterbury, July 9, 1951, 664.

96. Raley and Raley Flotte, *Images of America*, 72–73.

97. Raley and Raley Flotte, *Images of America*, 72–73.

98. Kaplan, *Zora Neale Hurston*, 605.

99. McCollum's experiences have been chronicled in books and documentaries as well as a Thulani Davis play. For more, see Huie, *Ruby McCollum*; Marks, Review of *In Black and White*.

100. Huie, *Ruby McCollum*.

101. Hurston to Hughes, May 31, 1929, 145.

102. Hurston to Jean Parker Waterbury, August 8, 1951, in Kaplan, *Zora Neale Hurston*, 673.

103. George Smathers to Zora Neale Hurston, October 25, 1954, Zora Neale Hurston Papers, Box 2, Folder 6, Special and Area Collections, George A. Smathers Libraries, University of Florida.

AFTERWORD

1. Preston, "Lost City Discovered in the Honduran Rain Forest."

2. Anderson, "The Complicated Career of Hugh Smythe."

3. The illustration is titled "Laguna—Puerto Cortés." Union Postal Universal, a branch of the United Nations, produced it.

4. Scutts, "The Woman Who Changed the Game for Black Writers."

5. West also launched *New Challenge*, a second magazine. Hurston to Dorothy West, March 24, 1934, in Kaplan, *Zora Neale Hurston*, 296. For more, see Durham, "Dorothy West and the Importance of Little 'Black' Magazines of the 1930s."

6. Kaplan, *Zora Neale Hurston*, 296.

7. Kaplan, *Zora Neale Hurston*, 296.

8. West, *The Wedding*.

9. Langston Hughes to Arna Bontemps, February 18, 1959, in Nichols, *Arna Bontemps Langston Hughes Letters*, 302.

10. Hughes to Bontemps, February 18, 1959, 302.

11. Hughes to Bontemps, February 18, 1959, 302.

12. Arna Bontemps to Langston Hughes, November 14, 1945, in Nichols, *Arna Bontemps Langston Hughes Letters*, 323.

13. Langston Hughes to Arna Bontemps, April 23, 1963, in Nichols, *Arna Bontemps Langston Hughes Letters*, 461.

14. Hurston to Charlotte Osgood Mason, December 20, 1930, in Kaplan, *Zora Neale Hurston*, 198.

15. Hurston to Mason, December 20, 1930, 198.

16. Hurston to Everett and Ivy Hurston, January 8, 1957, in Kaplan, *Zora Neale Hurston*, 750.

17. Hurston to Everett and Ivy Hurston, January 8, 1957, 750.

18. Hurston to Everett Edward Hurston, March 31, 1957, in Kaplan, *Zora Neale Hurston*, 752.

19. Kaplan, *Zora Neale Hurston*, 784.

20. Kaplan, *Zora Neale Hurston*, 784.

21. Kaplan, *Zora Neale Hurston*, 784.

22. Hurston to Langston Hughes, November 2, 1929, in Kaplan, *Zora Neale Hurston*, 153.

23. Perry, *Looking for Lorraine*, 22, 35–40.

24. Perry, *Looking for Lorraine*, 35.

25. Hurston to Claude Barnett, February 25, 1939, in Kaplan, *Zora Neale Hurston*, 421; Hurston to Barnett, February 25, 1939, 421. See also Hurston to unknown recipient, May 9, 1956, in Kaplan, *Zora Neale Hurston*, 748.

26. Hurston to Langston Hughes, July 23, 1929; Hurston to Langston Hughes, January 18, 1931; Hurston to Edwin Osgood Grover, November 7, 1943; Hurston to Everett Edward Hurston, March 31, 1957, in Kaplan, *Zora Neale Hurston*, 146, 201–204, 495, and 751.

27. Boyd, *Wrapped in Rainbows*, 414; Hurston to Jean Parker Waterbury, March 6, 1952, in Kaplan, *Zora Neale Hurston*, 682.

28. Edmund Morgan, Oscar Handlin, Theodore Allen, Lerone Bennett, Nikhil Pal Singh, Kathleen M. Brown, and Claire Robertson are among the researchers who have examined the issue of race and gender as social constructions. Two important works that address these subjects are Morgan, *Laboring Women*; and Roediger, *The Wages of Whiteness*.

29. Morgan, *Laboring Women*, 44–45; White, *Ar'n't I a Woman*, 7.

30. The 2018 scandal was tied to a discovery that some West Indians in the UK who had arrived before 1973 were wrongfully denied public services and, in some cases, subsequently deported. Noronha, *Deporting Black Britons*.

31. Noronha, *Deporting Black Britons*, 78.

32. Evans, *26a*, 11.

BIBLIOGRAPHY

ARCHIVES

Curt Teich Postcard Archives Collection, Newberry Library.
Edward E. Ayer Manuscript Collection, Newberry Library.
George Smathers Papers, Department of Special and Area Studies Collections, George A. Smathers Libraries, University of Florida.
Map Collection, Library of Congress.

PUBLICATIONS

Adichie, Chimamanda Ngozi. *Americanah*. New York: Alfred A.
Knopf, 2013.
Akhtar, Ayad. *Homeland Elegies: A Novel*. New York: Little, Brown, 2020.
Alonzo, Gualberto Zapata. *An Overview of the Mayan World with Synthesis
of the Olmec, Totonac, Zapotec, Mixtec, Teotihuacan, Toltec and Aztec
Civilizations*. Merida: Gualberto Zapta Alonzo, 1983.
Anderson, Mark. *Black and Indigenous: Garifuna Activism and Consumer Culture in Honduras*. Minneapolis: University of Minnesota
Press, 2009.
———. "The Complicated Career of Hugh Smythe . . . Anthropologist and
Ambassador: The Early Years, 1940–50." *Transforming Anthropology*
16, no. 2 (2008): 128–146.
Andrews, E. Wyllys, V. *Research and Reflections in Archaeology and History: Essays in Honor of Doris Stone*. New Orleans: Middle American
Research Institute, 1986.
Andrews, Sharony. "Festival for Black Author Reawakens Town to
Genius." *Miami Herald*, January 30, 1990, 1C.
———. "Fructifero, Emocionante Dialogo Aristide-Suarez." *El Nuevo
Herald*, September 28, 1991, 3B.
Banner, Lois W. *Intertwined Lives: Margaret Mead, Ruth Benedict, and
Their Circle*. New York: Alfred A. Knopf, 2003.

Basalla, Susan E. "Family Resemblances: Zora Neale Hurston's Anthropological Heritage." PhD diss., Princeton University, 1997.

Bassnett, Susan. "Travel Writing and Gender." In *The Cambridge Companion to Travel Writing*, edited by Peter Hulme and Tim Youngs, 225–241. Cambridge: Cambridge University Press, 2002.

Beaudry-Corbett, Marilyn, and Ellen T. Hardy, eds. *Early Scholars' Visits to Central America: Reports by Karl Sapper, Walter Lehmann, and Franz Termer*. Translated by Theodor E. Gutman. Los Angeles: Cotsen Institute of Archaeology, 2000.

Beeler, John. *Milne Papers*. Vol. 1: *The Papers of Admiral of the Fleet Sir Alexander Milne, Bt., K.C.B. (1806–1896)*. London: Ashgate for the Navy Records Society, 2004.

———. *Milne Papers*. Vol. 2: *The Royal Navy and the Outbreak of the American Civil War, 1860–1862*. Brookfield, VT: Ashgate Press for the Navy Records Society, 2015.

Beinecke Rare Book and Manuscript Library. "Biography Symposium: Ruth Franklin and Imani Perry." Accessed February 25, 2021. https://beinecke.library.yale.edu/event/biography-symposium-ruth-franklin-imani-perry.

Bell, Jonathan W. "Conceptualising Southern Liberalism: Ideology and the Pepper-Smathers 1950 Primary in Florida." *Journal of American Studies* 37, no. 1 (April 2003): 17–45.

Benjamin, Medea, ed. and trans. *Don't Be Afraid, Gringo: A Honduran Woman Speaks from the Heart; The Story of Elvia Alvarado*. San Francisco: Institute for Food and Development Policy, 1987.

Bennett, Victor W., and Barton A. Westerlund. *A Survey of the Winter Tourist Industry of Greater Miami, 1950*. n.p., n.d.

Bethell, Leslie, ed. *Central America since Independence*. New York: Cambridge University Press, 1991.

Bindas, Kenneth J. *Remembering the Great Depression in the Rural South*. Gainesville: University Press of Florida, 2007.

Binggeli, Elizabeth. "The Unadapted: Warner Bros. Reads Zora Neale Hurston." *Cinema Journal* 48, no. 3 (Spring 2009): 1–15.

Blumenschein, Marian. *Home in Honduras*. Independence, MO: Herald, 1975.

Bohls, Elizabeth A. *Women Travel Writers and the Language of Landscape Aesthetics, 1716–1818*. Cambridge: Cambridge University Press, 1995.

Bolster, W. Jeffrey. *Black Jacks: African American Seamen in the Age of Sail*. Cambridge, MA: Harvard University Press, 1997.

Bontemps, Arna. "From Eatonville, Florida to Harlem." *New York Herald Tribune*, November 22, 1942.

Boyd, Valerie. *Wrapped in Rainbows: The Life of Zora Neale Hurston*. New York: Lisa Drew Books, 2004.

Bradley, Regina. Zoom presentation, February 26, 2021, hosted by the University of Alabama's Gender and Race Studies Department.

Brady, Scott Arlen. "Honduras' Transisthmian Corridor: An Historical Geography of Road Building in Colonial Central America." PhD diss., Department of Geography and Anthropology, Louisiana State University, 1996

Brock, Lisa, and Digna Castaneda Fuertes, eds. *Between Race and Empire: African Americans and Cubans before the Cuban Revolution*. Philadelphia: Temple University Press, 1998.

Brown, Allen. "'Dying of Cold': ICE Detainees Freezing in Southern Prisons." *Intercept*, February 19, 2021. https://theintercept.com/2021/02/19/ice-detention-cold-freezing-texas-louisiana/.

Brown, Canter, Jr. *Florida's Black Public Officials, 1867–1924*. Tuscaloosa: University of Alabama Press, 1998.

Brunhouse, Robert L. *In Search of the Maya: The First Archaeologists*. Albuquerque: University of New Mexico Press, 1973.

Campbell-Copeland, Thomas, and María Soltera. *American Colonial Handbook: A Ready Reference Book of Facts and Figures*. London: Funk & Wagnalls, 1899.

Campt, Tina. *Listening to Images*. Durham, NC: Duke University Press, 2017.

Carby, Hazel V. *Imperial Intimacies: A Tale of Two Islands*. New York: Verso, 2019.

———. "The Politics of Fiction, Anthropology and the Folk: Zora Neale Hurston." In *New Essays on Their Eyes Were Watching God*, edited by Michael Awkward, 71–93. Cambridge: Cambridge University Press, 1990.

Carnes, Thomas L. *The Failure of Union: Central America, 1824–1960*. Chapel Hill: University of North Carolina Press, 2012.

Castañeda, Hilda de. *Beautiful Honduras: Experiences in a Small Town on the Caribbean*. London: Arthur H. Stockwell, 1900.

Cecelski, David S. *The Waterman's Song: Slavery and Freedom in Maritime North Carolina*. Chapel Hill: University of North Carolina Press, 2001.

Charles, John C. "Talk about the South: Unspeakable Things Unspoken in Zora Neale Hurston's 'Seraph on the Suwanee.'" *Mississippi Quarterly* 62, no. 1 (Winter 2009): 19–52.

Chambers, Glenn A. *Race, Nation and West Indian Immigration to Honduras, 1890–1940*. Baton Rouge: Louisiana State University Press, 2010.

Chapman, Peter. *Bananas: How the United Fruit Company Shaped the World*. New York: Canongate, 2008.

Chomsky, Aviva, and Aldo Lauria-Santiago, eds. *Identity and Struggle at the Margins of the Nation-State: The Laboring Peoples of Central America and the Hispanic Caribbean*. Durham, NC: Duke University Press, 1998.

Clark, James C. *Red Pepper and Gorgeous George: Claude Pepper's Epic Defeat in the 1950 Democratic Primary*. Gainesville: University Press of Florida, 2011.

Coe, Michael D. *The Maya*. 7th ed. New York: Thames and Hudson, 2005.

Cohen, Rich. *The Fish That Ate the Whale: The Life and Times of America's Banana King*. New York: Picador, 2013.

Cohn, Nate. "Why Warnock and Ossoff Won in Georgia." *New York Times*, January 7, 2021.

Colby, Jason M. *The Business of Empire: United Fruit, Race and U.S. Expansion*. Ithaca, NY: Cornell University Press, 2013.

Cordingly, David. *Women Sailors and Sailors' Women: An Untold Maritime History*. New York: Random House, 2001.

Crispell, Brian Lewis. *Testing the Limits: George Armstead Smathers and Cold War America*. Athens: University of Georgia Press, 1999.

Culbert, T. Patrick. *The Lost Civilization: The Story of the Classic Maya*. New York: Harper & Row, 1974.

Davidson, William V. *Etnología y etnohistoria de Honduras: Ensayos* [Ethnology and ethnohistory of Honduras: Essays].Tegucigalpa: Instituto Hondureno de Antropologia e Historia, 2008.

———. *The Lost Towns of Honduras*. Memphis, TN: William V. Davidson, 2017.

de la Fuente, Alejandro, and George R. Andrews, eds. *Estudios Afrolatinoamericanos: Una Introducción*. Harvard, CLASCO, 2018.

de la Fuente, Alejandro, and Ariela J. Gross. *Becoming Free, Becoming Black: Race, Freedom and Law in Cuba, Virginia and Louisiana*. Cambridge: Cambridge University Press, 2020.

Dickinson, Joyce Wallace. "Florida's Senatorial Slugfest Was Bitter, Ugly, Legendary." *Orlando Sentinel*, September 24, 2000. www.orlandosentinel.com/news/os-xpm-2000-09-24-0009230163-story.html.

Diner, Hasia, Shira Kohn, and Rachel Kranson, eds. *A Jewish Feminine Mystique? Jewish Women in Postwar America*. New Brunswick, NJ: Rutgers University Press, 2010.

Dodd, Thomas J. *Tiburcio Carías: Portrait of a Honduran Political Leader*. Baton Rouge: Louisiana State University, 2005.

Douglas, Frederick. *Frederick Douglass: Autobiographies; Narrative of the Life of Frederick Douglass, an American Slave / My Bondage and My Freedom / Life and Times of Frederick Douglass.* Edited by Henry Louis Gates Jr. Boone, IA: Library of America, 1994.

——. *Life and Times of Frederick Douglass.* n.p., 1881.

——. *My Bondage and My Freedom.* Edited by David Blight. 1855; New Haven, CT: Yale University Press, 2014.

——. *Narrative of the Life of Frederick Douglass, an American Slave.* 1845; Simon & Brown, 2013.

Dubeck, Laura. "The Social Geography of Race in Hurston's *Seraph on the Suwanee.*" *African American Review* 30 (Fall 1996): 341–351.

Dunn, Marvin. *Black Miami in the Twentieth Century.* Gainesville: University Press of Florida, 1997.

Durham, Joyce. "Dorothy West and the Importance of Little 'Black' Magazines of the 1930s: 'Challenge' and 'New Challenge.'" *Langston Hughes Review* 16, nos. 1/2 (Fall/Spring 1999–2001): 19–31.

Dym, Jordana, and Karl Offen. *Mapping Latin America: A Cartographic Reader.* Chicago: University of Chicago Press, 2011.

Emmrich, Stuart. "Has the Oscars Race Already Narrowed to *Nomadland* and *One Night in Miami?*" *Vogue,* September 26, 2020. www.vogue.com/article/oscar-predictions-2021.

England, Sarah. *Afro Central Americans in New York City: Garifuna Tales of Transnational Movements in Racialized Space.* Gainesville: University Press of Florida, 2006.

Euraque, Darío A. "The Banana Enclave, Nationalism, and Mestizaje in Honduras, 1910–1930s." In *Identity and Struggle at the Margins of the Nation-State: The Laboring Peoples of Central America and the Hispanic Caribbean,* edited by Aviva Chomsky and Aldo Lauria-Santiago. Durham, NC: Duke University Press, 1998.

——. *Reinterpreting the Region and State in the Banana Republic, Honduras 1870–1972.* Chapel Hill: University of North Carolina Press, 1996.

Euraque, Dario A., and Yesenia Martinez. *The African Diaspora in the Educational Programs of Central America.* Trenton, NJ: Africa World Press, 2016.

Evans, Diana. *26a.* New York: Harper Perennial, 2006.

Fanon, Frantz. *Wretched of the Earth.* New York: Grove Press, 1963.

Fasquelle, Ricardo Agurcia. "Snakes, Jaguars, and Outlaws: Some Comments on Central American Archaeology." In *Research and Reflections in Archaeology and History: Essays in Honor of Doris Stone,* edited by E. Wyllys Andrews V. New Orleans: Middle American Research Institute, 1986.

Fay, Marianne, and Mary Morrison. *Infrastructure in Latin America and the Caribbean: Recent Developments and Key Challenges*. Washington, DC: World Bank, 2007.

Federal Writers' Project. *Florida: A Guide to the Southernmost State*. New York: Oxford University Press, 1939.

Findlay, Eileen J. Suarez. *Imposing Decency: The Politics of Sexuality and Race in Puerto Rico, 1870–1920*. Durham, NC: Duke University Press, 1999.

Finkelstein, David. *The House of Blackwood: Author-Publisher Relations in the Victorian Age* University Park: Pennsylvania University Press, 2002.

———, ed. *Print Culture and the Blackwood Tradition 1805–1930*. Toronto: University of Toronto Press, 2006.

Fisher, Jane. *Fabulous Hoosier: A Story of American Achievement*. Chicago: Harry Coleman, 1953.

Floyd, Troy S. *The Anglo-Spanish Struggle for Mosquitia*. Albuquerque: University of New Mexico Press, 1970.

Foner, Philip S. *Antonio Maceo: The "Bronze Titan" of Cuba's Struggle for Independence*. New York: Monthly Review Press, 1977.

Foster-Frau, Silvia, and Arelis R. Hernández. "Freezing Temperatures and Power Outages Leave Texas's Most Vulnerable yet Again." *Washington Post*, February 16, 2021. www.washingtonpost.com/national/texas-storm-hurts-most-vulnerable-again/2021/02/16/fe3c8fd4–707b-11eb-93be-c10813e358a2_story.html.

"Frederick Koch, 88, Who Found a New Way to Stage Theater." *New York Times*, September 15, 2000. www.nytimes.com/2000/09/15/arts/frederick-koch-88-who-found-a-new-way-to-stage-theater.html.

Fujiwara, Chris. *The Cinema of Nightfall: Jacques Tourneur*. Baltimore: John Hopkins University Press, 1998.

Gauthier, H. L. "Highway Transportation and Regional Development in South America." In *Latin America: Case Studies*, edited by Richard G. Boehm and Sent Visser, 175–86. Dubuque, IA: Kendall Hunt, 1984.

George, Lynell. *A Handful of Earth, a Handful of Sky: The World of Octavia E. Butler*. Santa Monica, CA: Angel City Press, 2020.

Gibson, Thelma Vernell. *Forbearance: The Life Story of a Coconut Grove Native*. Homestead, FL: Helena Enterprises, 2000.

Glassman, Steve, and Kathryn Lee Seidel. *Zora in Florida*. Orlando: University of Central Florida Press, 1991.

Gonzalez-Tennant, Edward. *The Rosewood Massacre: An Archaeology and History of Intersectional Violence*. Gainesville: University Press of Florida, 2018.

Gordon, Deborah. "The Politics of Ethnographic Authority: Race and Writing in the Ethnography of Margaret Mead and Zora Neale Hurston." In *Modernist Anthropology*, 146–62. Princeton, NJ: Princeton University Press, 1990.

Green, Sharony Andrews. *Cuttin' the Rug under the Moonlit Sky: Stories and Drawings about a Bunch of Women Named Mae*. New York: Anchor, 1997.

———. *Grant Green: Rediscovering the Forgotten Genius of Jazz Guitar*. San Francisco: Miller Freeman, 1999.

———. *Remember Me to Miss Louisa: Hidden Black-White Intimacies in Antebellum America*. DeKalb: Northern Illinois University Press, 2015.

———. "Tracing Black Racial and Spatial Politics in South Florida via Memory." *Journal of Urban History* 44, no. 6 (November 2018): 1176–1196. First published January 30, 2017.

———. "When I First Wore Fish Leather, or Black Girl in Iceland." In *Pan African Spaces: Essays on Black Transnationalism*, edited by Msia Kibona Clark, Loy Azalia, and Phiwokuhle Mynandu, 61–70. Lanham, MD: Lexington Books, 2019.

Gudmundson, Lowell, and Justin Wolfe, eds. *Blacks and Blackness in Central America*. Durham, NC: Duke University Press, 2010.

Guterl, Matthew Pratt. *American Mediterranean: Southern Slaveholders in the Age of Emancipation*. Cambridge, MA: Harvard University Press, 2008.

Harrison, Camira. "Once Bastion for Blacks, Bethune Beach Named Historic Site." *Daytona Beach News-Journal*, May 19, 2017. www.newsjournalonline.com/news/20170519/once-bastion-for-blacks-bethune-beach-named-historic-site.

Hartman, Saidiya. *Lose Your Mother: A Journey Along the Atlantic Slave Route*. New York: Farrar, Straus and Giroux, 2006.

Hassall, Kathleen. "Text and Personality in Disguise and in the Open: Zora Neale Hurston's *Dust Tracks on a Road*." In *Zora in Florida*, edited by Steve Glassman and Kathryn Lee Seidel, 159–73. Orlando: University of Central Florida, 1991.

Helg, Aline. *Liberty and Equality in Caribbean Colombia, 1770–1835*. Chapel Hill: University of North Carolina Press, 2004.

Hemenway, Robert. *Zora Neale Hurston: A Literary Biography*. Urbana: University of Illinois Press, 1977.

Henry, O. *Cabbages and Kings*. New York: Doubleday, 1904.

Hernandez, Graciela. "Multiple Subjectivities and Strategic Positionality: Zora Neale Hurston's Experimental Ethnographies." In *Women*

Writing and Culture, edited by Ruth Behar and Deborah A. Gordon. Berkeley: University of California Press, 1995.

Hobbs, Maurice. *The Legend of the Black Mecca: Politics and Class in the Making of Modern Atlanta*. Chapel Hill: University of North Carolina Press, 2017.

Hofstadter, Richard. "The Paranoid Style in American Politics." *Harper's*, November 1964. https://harpers.org/archive/1964/11/the-paranoid-style-in-american-politics/.

Hollar, B. J. *Thirteen Loops: Race, Violence, and the Last Lynching in America*. Tuscaloosa: University of Alabama Press, 2011.

Horton, James Oliver, and Stacy Flaherty. "Black Leadership in Antebellum Cincinnati." In *Race and the City: Work, Community, and Protest in Cincinnati, 1820–1970*, edited by Henry Louis Taylor Jr. Urbana: University of Illinois Press, 1993.

Howard-Regundin, Pamela F. *Honduras*. Vol. 139 in *World Bibliographic Series*. Oxford: Clio Press, 1992.

Hughes, Langston. *The Big Sea: An Autobiography*. New York: Hill and Wang, 1940, 1993.

Huie, William Bradford. *Ruby McCollum: Woman in the Suwannee Jail*. New York: E. P. Dutton, 1956.

Hurston, Lucy Ann, and the estate of Zora Neale Hurston. *Speak So You Can Speak Again: The Life of Zora Neale Hurston*. New York: Doubleday, 2004.

Hurston, Zora Neale. *Barracoon: The Story of the Last "Black Cargo."* New York: Amistad, 2018.

———. *Dust Tracks on a Road*. New York: Harper Perennial, 1942, 2006.

———. "How It Feels to Be Colored Me." In *I Love Myself When I Am Laughing . . . and Then Again When I Am Looking Mean and Impressive: A Zora Neale Hurston Reader*, edited by Alice Walker. New York: Feminist Press at City University of New York, 1979, 2020.

———. "I Saw Negro Votes Peddled." *American Legion*, November 1950.

———. "The Pet Negro System." *American Mercury*, May 1943. Reprinted in *Zora Neale Hurston: Folklore, Memoirs, and Other Writings*, ed. Cheryl Wall. New York: Library of American, 1995.

———. *Seraph on the Suwanee*. New York: Perennial, 1948, 1991.

———. *Tell My Horse: Voodoo and Life in Haiti and Jamaica*. New York: Harper Perennial, 1938, 1990.

———. *Their Eyes Were Watching God*. Urbana: University of Illinois Press, 1937, 1991.

———. "What White Publishers Won't Print." In *Within the Circle: African American Literary Criticism from the Harlem Renaissance to the*

Present, edited by Angelyn Mitchell. Durham, NC: Duke University Press, 1994.

Hurston, Zora Neale, Henry Louis Gates Jr., and M. Genevieve West. *You Don't Know Us Negroes and Other Essays*. New York: Amistad, 2022.

Incidents of Travel in Central America, Chiapas and Yucatán. Vols. 1 and 2. New York: Cambridge University Press, 1841, 2010.

Jackson, Chuck. "Waste and Whiteness: Zora Neale Hurston and the Politics of Eugenics." *African American Review* (Winter 2000): 639–659.

Jacoby, Susan. "The 350,000 Cubans in South Florida Make a Remarkable Success Story: Even If Castro Fell Tomorrow, Great Numbers Would Not Return." *New York Times*, September 29, 1974.

Jelly-Schapiro, Joshua. *Island People: The Caribbean and the World*. New York: Alfred A. Knopf, 2016.

Jennings, A. J. *Through the Shadows with O. Henry*. New York: A. L. Burt, 1921.

Johnson, Paul Christopher. *Diaspora Conversion: Black Carib Region and the Recovery of Africa*. Berkeley: University of California Press, 2007.

Jolly, Ricky. *Jackspeak: A Guide to British Naval Slang and Usage*. Oxford: Osprey, 1989, 2011.

Jones, Howard. *My Lai: Vietnam, 1968, and the Descent into Darkness*. New York: Oxford University Press, 2017.

Kaplan, Carla, ed. *Zora Neale Hurston: A Life in Letters*. New York: Anchor, 2002.

Keeling, David J. "Latin America's Transportation Conundrum." *Journal of Latin American Geography* 7, no. 2 (2008): 133–154.

Kelly, James. "South Florida, Trouble in Paradise." *Time*, November 23, 1981.

Kennedy, David M. *The American People in the Great Depression: Freedom from Fear Part One*. New York: Oxford University Press, 2003.

King, Charles. *Gods of the Upper Air: How a Circle of Renegade Anthropologists Reinvented Race, Sex and Gender in the Twentieth Century*. New York, Anchor, 2019.

LaFeber, Walter. *Inevitable Revolutions: The United States in Central America*. New York: W. W. Norton, 1983.

Lambert, Andrew. *Crusoe's Island: A Rich and Curious History of Pirates, Castaways and Madness*. London: Faber & Faber, 2017.

Lange, Frederick W. "Central America and the Southwest: A Comparison of Mesoamerica's Two Peripheries." In *Research and Reflections in Archaeology and History: Essays in Honor of Doris Stone*, edited by E. Wyllys Andrews V, 159–77. New Orleans: Middle American Research Institute, 1986.

Lara, José I. "Gendered National Bodies & Racial Difference in *A Lady's Ride across Spanish Honduras.*" *Humanities Bulletin* 1, no. 2 (November 2018): 205–221.

Lazo, Rodrigo. "Come Party to Goombay's Hopping Beat." *Miami Herald*, June 4, 1989, 1B.

Ledger, Sally, and Holly Furneaux, eds. *Charles Dickens in Context.* Cambridge: Cambridge University Press, 2011.

Lipsitz, George. "The Racialization of Space and the Spatialization of Race: Theorizing the Hidden Architecture of Landscape." *Landscape Journal* 26, no. 1 (2007): 10–23.

Lipsytes, Robert. "Clay Discusses His Future, Liston and Black Muslims." *New York Times*, February 27, 1964, 34.

List of United States Citizens for Immigration Authorities. Microfilm Serial: T715, 1897–1957, www.ancestry.com.

Lovell, Mary S. *A Rage to Live: A Biography of Richard and Isabel Burton.* New York: W. W. Norton, 1998.

Lowe, John. *Jump at the Sun: Zora Neale Hurston's Cosmic Comedy.* Urbana: University of Illinois Press, 1994.

Luke, Bob, and John David Smith. *Soldiering for Freedom: How the Union Army Recruited, Trained, and Deployed the U.S. Colored Troops.* Baltimore: Johns Hopkins University Press, 2014.

Lyons, Angela, Haskins & Sells Foundation, and American Institute of Accountants. "Public Practice of Accounting in the Republic of Honduras" (1951). Haskins and Sells Publications, 1770. https://egrove.olemiss.edu/dl_hs/1770.

Lyons, James. "Famous Negro Author Working as a Maid Here Just 'to Live a Little.'" *Miami Herald*, March 27, 1950, 1-B.

Maass, Harold, Sharony Andrews, and Arnold Markowitz. "Passions Flame Up in Little Haiti." *Miami Herald*, October 1, 1991, 1A.

Mack, T. "Contraband Trade through Trujillo, Honduras," 1720s–1782." *Yearbook, Conference of Latin Americanist Geographers* 24 (1998): 44–56.

MacRae Taylor, Douglas. *The Black Carib of British Honduras.* New York: Wenner-Gren Foundation for Anthropological Research, 1963.

Marks, Peter. Review of *In Black and White: Cold Blood or Hot Rage, New York Times*, March 10, 1999. www.nytimes.com/1999/03/10/theater/theater-review-in-black-and-white-cold-blood-or-hot-rage.html.

Mattison, Hiram, and Louisa Picquet. *The Octoroon: A Tale of Southern Slave Life.* New York: Author, 1861.

McGovern, James R. *Anatomy of a Lynching: The Killing of Claude Neal.* Baton Rouge: Louisiana State University Press, 1992.

McKillop Wells, Marilyn. *Among the Garifuna: Family Tales and Ethnography from the Caribbean Coast*. Tuscaloosa: University of Alabama Press, 2015.

McKittrick, Katherine. *Dear Science and Other Stories*. Durham, NC: Duke University Press, 2021.

McNealey, Earnestine Green. *Pearls of Service: The Legacy of America's First Black Sorority, Alpha Kappa Alpha*. Chicago: Alpha Kappa Alpha Sorority, 2006.

Mehren, Elizabeth. "A Haunting Death Inspires 'Beloved': Novelist Morrison Writes of Families, Freedom and Slavery." *Los Angeles Times*, October 14, 1987. https://www.latimes.com/archives/la-xpm-1987-10-14-vw-9326-story.html.

Mercer, Wendy S. "Gender and Genre in Nineteenth Century Travel Writing: Leone d'Aunet and Xavier Marmier." In *Travel Writing and Empire: Postcolonial Theory in Transit*, edited by Steven H. Clark, 147–163. London: Zeb Book, 1999.

Miami Herald. Obituary, Rev. Constance Mary Lang. May 26, 2004.

Mikell, Gwendolyn. "The Anthropological Imagination of Zora Neale Hurston." *Western Journal of Black Studies* 7, no. 1 (1983): 27–35.

Mills, Sara. *Discourses of Difference: An Analysis of Women's Travel Writing and Colonialism*. London: Routledge, 1999.

Mohl, Raymond A. "'South of the South?': Jews, Blacks, and the Civil Rights Movement in Miami, 1945–1960." *Journal of American Ethnic History* 18, no. 2 (Winter 1999): 3–36.

Mohl, Raymond A., Matilda "Bobbi" Graff, and Shirley M. Zoloth. *South of the South: Jewish Activists and the Civil Rights Movement in Miami, 1945–1960*. Gainesville: University Press of Florida, 2004.

Morgan, Jennifer L. *Laboring Women: Reproduction and Gender in New World Slavery*. Philadelphia: University of Pennsylvania Press, 2004.

Mormino, Gary R. "Florida Slave Narratives." *Florida Historical Quarterly* 66, no. 4 (1988): 399–419.

Moylan, Virginia Lynn. *Zora Neale Hurston's Final Decade*. Gainesville: University Press of Florida, 2011.

Nathiri, N. Y., ed. *Zora Neale Hurston: A Woman and Her Community*. Orlando: Sentinel, 1991.

National Public Radio. "Childhood Playmates Reconnect, Rekindle Friendship that Transcends Race and Distance." *Weekend Edition*, March 18, 2018. www.npr.org/2018/03/18/594671317/reconnecting-with-childhood-friends.

Nations, James D. *The Maya Tropical Forest: People, Parks and Ancient Cities*. Austin: University of Texas Press, 2006.

Naylor, Robert A. *Penny Ante Imperialism: The Mosquito Shore and the Bay of Honduras, 1600–1924; A Case Study in British Informal Empire*. Rutherford: Fairleigh Dickinson University Press, 1989.

Neptune, Harvey R. *Caliban and the Yankees: Trinidad and the United States Occupation*. Chapel Hill: University of North Carolina Press, 2007.

Nguyen, Viet Thanh. *The Sympathizer*. New York: Grove Press, 2015.

Nicholls, David G. "Migrant Labor, Folklore, and Resistance in Hurston's Polk County: Reframing Mules and Men." *African American Review* 33, no. 3 (1999): 467–479.

Nichols, Charles H., ed. *Arna Bontemps Langston Hughes Letters, 1925–1967*. New York: Penguin, 1990.

Nijman, Jan. *Miami: Mistress of the Americas*. Philadelphia: University of Pennsylvania Press, 2011.

Noronha, Luke de. *Deporting Black Britons: Portraits of Deportation to Jamaica*. Manchester: Manchester University Press, 2020.

Ogle, Maureen. *Key West: History of an Island of Dreams*. Gainesville: University of Press of Florida, 2006.

Otis, John. "Colombian's President on Amnesty for Venezuelans: 'We Want to Set an Example.'" National Public Radio, March 3, 2021. www.npr.org/2021/03/03/972907206/colombias-president-on-amnesty-for-venezuelans-we-want-to-set-an-example.

Parker, Idella, with Mary Keating. *Idella: Marjorie Rawlins' "Perfect Maid."* Gainesville: University Press of Florida, 1992.

Parker, Marjorie H. *Past Is Prologue: The History of Alpha Kappa Alpha 1908–1999*. Chicago: Alpha Kappa Alpha Sorority, 1999.

Pattee, Fred Lewis. Preface to *American Writers: A Series of Papers Contributed to Blackwood's Magazine (1824–1825)*, edited by Fred Lewis Pattee, n.p. Durham, NC: Duke University Press, 1937.

Peckenham, Nancy, and Annie Street, eds. *Honduras: Portrait of a Captive Nation*. New York, Praeger, 1985.

Perry, Imani. *Looking for Lorraine: The Radiant Life of Lorraine Hansberry*. Boston: Beacon Press, 2018.

Peters, Pearlie Mae Fisher. *The Assertive Woman in Zora Neale Hurston's Fiction, Folklore and Drama*. New York: Garland, 1998.

Plant, Deborah G. *Every Tub Must Sit on Its Own Bottom: The Philosophy and Politics of Zora Neale Hurston*. Urbana: University of Illinois Press, 1995.

Porter, Kimberly K. "Editor's Introduction." *Oral History Review* 34, no. 2 (2007): vii–viii.

Potter, Eliza. *A Hairdresser's Experience in High Life.* 1859; New York: Oxford University Press, 1991.

Pratt, Mary Louise. *Imperial Eyes and Transculturation.* London: Routledge, 1992.

Preston, Douglas. "Exclusive: Lost City Discovered in the Honduran Rain Forest." *National Geographic*, March 2, 2015.

Putnam, Lara. *Radical Moves: Caribbean Migrants and the Politics of Race in the Jazz Age.* Chapel Hill: University of North Carolina Press, 2013.

Raley, Karen, and Ann Raley Flotte. *Images of America: Melbourne and Eau Gallie.* Charleston: Acadia, 2002.

Rey Rosa, Rodrigo. *Dust on Her Tongue.* Translated by Paul Bowles. San Francisco: City Lights Books, 1992.

Richardson, Joe. *African Americans in the Reconstruction of Florida, 1865–1877.* Tuscaloosa: University of Alabama Press, 1965.

Rieger, Christopher. "The Working-Class Pastoral of Zora Neale Hurston's 'Seraph on the Suwanee.'" *Mississippi Quarterly* 56, no. 1 (Winter 2002–2003): 105–124.

Roediger, David. *The Sinking Middle Class: A Political History.* New York: OR Books, 2020.

Roediger, David R. *The Wages of Whiteness: Race and the Making of the American Working Class.* Brooklyn: Verso, 1991.

Romney, D. H. *Land in British Honduras: Report of the British Honduras Land Use Survey.* London: Her Majesty's Stationery Office, 1959.

Rose, Chanelle Nyree. *The Struggle for Freedom in Black Miami: Civil Rights and America's Tourist Paradise, 1896–1968.* Baton Rouge: Louisiana State University Press, 2015.

Sandweiss, Martha A. *Passing Strange: A Gilded Age Tale of Love and Deception across the Color Line.* New York: Penguin, 2009.

Sarton, May. *Journal of a Solitude.* New York: W. W. Norton, 1973.

Schlicke, Paul. *The Oxford Companion to Charles Dickens.* Anniversary ed. Oxford: Oxford University Press, 2011.

Schulman, Bruce J. *The Seventies: The Great Shift in American Culture, Society and Politics.* New York: Da Capo Press, 2002.

Scottish Geographical Journal 50, no. 6 (1934).

Scutts, Joanna. "The Woman Who Changed the Game for Black Writers." *Time*, February 3, 2016. https://time.com/4199755/dorothy-west-history/.

Sears, Donald A. *John Neal.* Boston, MA: Twayne, 1979.

Selvon, Sam. *The Lonely Londoners.* Edinburgh: Pearson Education, 1956.

Shange, Ntozake. "Bocas: A Daughter's Geography." In *A Daughter's Geography*, 2–3. New York: St. Martin's Press, 1983.

Sheptak, Russell. "Mythical Ciudad Blanca." *Honduras Culture and Politics* (blog), May 20, 2012. http://hondurasculturepolitics.blogspot. com/2012/05/mythical-ciudad-blanca.html.

Shreitfeld, David. "Dorothy West, Renaissance Woman," *Washington Post*, July 6, 1995. www.washingtonpost.com/archive/ lifestyle/1995/07/06/dorothy-west-renaissance-woman/462a9c6e-e2e5-4a04-a082-6f923e4b40d4/.

Sierakowski, Robert. "Central America's Caribbean Coast: Politics and Ethnicity." *Oxford Research Encyclopedia, Latin American History.* September 29, 2016. https://oxfordre.com/latinamericanhistory/ view/10.1093/acrefore/9780199366439.001.0001/acrefore-9780199366439-e-372?rskey=FlSmFh&result=1.

Singletary, Otis A., and Jane P. Newman, eds. *American Universities and Colleges.* 10th ed. Washington, DC: American Council on Education, 1968.

Smith, John David, ed. *Black Soldiers in Blue: African American Troops in the Civil War Era.* Chapel Hill: University of North Carolina Press, 2002, 2004.

———. *Lincoln and the U.S. Colored Troops.* Carbondale: Southern Illinois University Press, 2013.

Smith, R. J. *The Great Black Way: L.A. in the 1940s and the Lost African American Renaissance.* New York: Public Affairs, 2006.

Smith, Teresa. "Love Beads and Squash Sold Here," *Miami Herald, Neighbors SE*, March 22, 1987, 18.

Smith, Zadie. *Swing Time.* New York: Penguin, 2016.

Soltera, María. *A Lady's Ride across Spanish Honduras.* Gainesville: University of Florida Press, 1964.

The South American Handbook. 27th annual ed. London: Trade & Travel, 1950.

St. Clair, Jane. "The Courageous Undertow of Zora's *Seraph on the Suwanee*." *Modern Language Quarterly* 50 (March 1989): 38–57.

Stuckey, Sterling. *Slave Culture: Nationalist Theory and the Foundations of Black America.* New York: Oxford University Press, 1987.

Stuelke, Patricia. *The Ruse of Repair: U.S. Neoliberal Empire and the Turn from Critique.* Durham, NC: Duke University Press, 2021.

———. "'Sympathy with the Swamp': Reading Hurston in the Trumpocene." *Scholar & Feminist Online* 16, no. 2 (2020). https://sfonline. barnard.edu/zora-neale-hurston/sympathy-with-the-swamp/.

———. "'Times when Greater Disciplines Are Born': The Zora Neale Hurston Revival and the Neoliberal Transformation of the Caribbean." *American Literature* 86, no. 1 (March 2014): 117–45.

Szwed, John. *So What: The Life of Miles Davis*. New York: Simon and Schuster, 2003.

Tate, Claudia. "Hitting 'a Straight Lick with a Crooked Stick': *Seraph on the Suwanee*, Zora Neale Hurston's Whiteface Novel." In *Psychoanalysis of Race*, edited by Christopher Lane. New York: Columbia University Press, 1998.

Thebault, Reis, Lewis Velarde, and Abigail Hauslohner. "The Father and Daughter Who Drowned at the Border Were Desperate for a Better Life, Family Says." *Washington Post*, June 26, 2019. www.washingtonpost.com/world/2019/06/26/father-daughter-who-drowned-border-dove-into-river-desperation/.

Thompson, Carl. *Travel Writing: A New Critical Idiom*. London: Taylor & Francis, 2011.

Thurman, Wallace. *Infants of the Spring*. 1932; New York: Dover, 2013.

Trollope, Frances. *Domestic Manners of the Americans*. Edited by Donald Smalley. 1832; Gloucester, MA: Peter Smith, 1974.

US Treasury Department, Bureau of Customs. *Merchant Vessels of the United States, 1949*. Washington, DC: US Government Printing Office, 1949.

Van Vechten, Carl. *Nigger Heaven*. New York: Alfred A. Knopf, 1926.

Volte, Luther. "Private Negro Housing Plan Called Hodge-Podge." *Miami Herald*, March 27, 1950, 1B.

Wagner, Tamara. "Travel Writing." In *Cambridge Companion to Victorian Women's Writings*, edited by Linda H. Peterson, 175–188. Cambridge: Cambridge University Press, 2015.

Walker, Alice. "Light a Candle for Raid Badawi." In *Taking the Arrow Out of the Heart*. New York: Atria, 2018.

Wall, Cheryl, ed. *Zora Neale Hurston: Folklore, Memoir and Other Writings*. New York: Library of American, 1995.

Wells, Williams V. *Explorations and Adventures in the Honduras*. New York: Harper & Brothers, 1857.

West, Dorothy. *The Wedding*. New York: Anchor, 1995, 1996.

White, Deborah Gray. *Ar'n't I a Woman: Female Slaves in the Plantation South*. New York: W. W. Norton, 1985.

Whitehead, Kevin. "Grant Green: The 'Holy Barbarian' of St. Louis Jazz." *Fresh Air*, January 11, 2013. www.npr.org/2013/01/11/169130324/grant-green-the-holy-barbarian-of-st-louis-jazz.

Wilkerson, Isabel. *The Warmth of Other Suns: The Epic Story of America's Great Migration*. Vintage: New York, 2010.

Wintz, Cary D. *Remember the Harlem Renaissance*. Abingdon: Taylor & Francis, 1996.

Writer's Program of the Works Progress Administration in the State of Florida, Guide to Key West. New York: Hastings House, 1941.

Yde, Jens. *An Archaeological Reconnaissance of Northwestern Honduras: A Report of the Work of the Tulane University–Danish National Museum Expedition to Central America, 1935*. Copenhagen: Levin & Munksgaard, 1938.

Young, Thomas. *Narrative of a Residence on the Mosquito Shore during the Years 1839, 1840 & 1841 with an Account of Truxillo, and the Adjacent Islands of Bonacca and Roatán*. London: Smith, Elder, 1842.

Zoloth, Shirley. "Miami Integration: Silence Causes Failure." *Southern Patriot* 17 (December 1959): 1–3.

MUSIC

Getz, Stan, and João Gilberto. "The Girl from Ipanema." Recorded March 18–19, 1963. *Getz/Gilberto*. Creed Taylor, Verve, 1964, vinyl.

Green, Grant. *Easy*. Recorded April 17–20, 1978. Versatile, 1978, vinyl.

———. *The Latin Bit*. Recorded April 26 and September 7, 1962. Blue Note, 1963, vinyl.

Simone, Nina. "My Sweet Lord / Today Is a Killer." Recorded 1971. *Emergency Ward*. RCA Victor, vinyl.

TLC. "Waterfalls." Recorded in 1993 and September 1994. *CrazySexyCool*. LaFace, Arista, 1994, CD.

TELECASTS / MOTION PICTURES

Appointment in Honduras. Jacques Tourneur, dir. 1953. New York, RKO, film.

Bananas. Woody Allen, dir. 1971. Hollywood, United Artists, film.

The Birdcage. Mike Nichols, dir. 1997. New York, United Artists, film.

Girls Trip. Malcolm D. Lee, dir. 2017. Universal Pictures, film.

The Mali-Cuba Connection. Richard Minier, dir. 2019. France, ArtMattan Films. www.imdb.com/title/tt10506096/, film.

The Mosquito Coast. Peter Weir, dir. 1986. Paul Zaentz / Warner Brothers, film.

The Mosquito Coast. Rupert Wyatt, dir. 2021. Freemantle/Apple, television drama.

Working Girl. Mike Nichols, dir. 1988. 20th Century Fox, film.

INDEX

Blumenschein, Marian, 15-17, 62, 75
Boas, Franz, 18, 24
Bontemps, Arna, 19, 20, 23, 24-25, 47, 48, 114
Botkin, Benjamin, 95
Boyd, Norma, 26, 134n17
Boyd, Valerie, xii, 49
Brett, Reginald, 31-32, 67
Brickell, Mary, 92
Brickell, William, 92
Brown v. Board of Education, 97
Burke, Edward, 115
Burton, Richard Francis, 66

Cabbages and Kings (O. Henry), 8
campesinos (peasants), 42-43, 74
Campt, Tina, 40
Carby, Hazel, 40, 54, 122
Carías Andino, Tiburcio, 4, 14
Caribbean Sea, 52
Castañeda, Hilda de, 10
Castro, Fidel, 144n34
Catherwood, Frederick, 56
Central America: animals and reptiles, 62-63; archaeological research, 60; attitude toward immigrants, 42; civil unrest in, 41-42; map of, 67; poverty in, 42-43; railway construction in, 56; status of women, 42-43; transportation problems, 16-17, 75-76; unification attempt, 69; wars in, 43-44
Challenge (magazine), 112
Challenger (schooner), 89, 91, 92
Charles, John, 49
Churchill, Winston, 4
Clay, Cassius, 93
Clotilda (ship), 28, 59, 135n33
Cocoa Beach, FL, 109
Cohen, Isadore, 92
Colombia: Venezuelan migrants in, 139n37
Columbia University, 6, 7, 18, 24, 31, 34, 87
Columbus, Christopher, 9, 60
Columbus, Ferdinand, 9
Comayagua, Honduras, 75, 77-78, 79
contras (counterrevolutionary fighters), 44
Cortés, Hernán, 9
Costa Rica, xiii, 9, 36, 42

Cracroft, Peter, 84
Creech, Sara Lee, 95
Creole people, 58
Crisis (journal), 73
Cuba: attitudes toward immigrants, 42; Bay of Pigs invasion, 42; hurricane in, 34; music studies in, 144n34; people of African descent in, 73; slavery in, 72-73
Cullen, Countee, 30

Dávila, Miguel, 41, 42
Daytona Beach, FL, 23, 25, 26, 35, 68
Don Guillermo (ship), 89
Douglass, Frederick, 27, 35
Du Bois, W. E. B., 20, 35, 116
Dust Tracks on a Road (Hurston), 19, 23, 133n115

Eaton, Josiah, xiv
Eatonville, FL, xiv, 21, 23, 30, 38
Eau Gallie, FL, 68, 106-9, 124
Ellington, Duke, 47
El Salvador, xiii, 6, 43, 67
Evans, Diana, 120

Fauset, Jessie, 47
Fisher, Carl, 92
Flagler, Henry, 92
Florida: culture of, 115; economy of, 25-26; Ku Klux Klan in, 102; map of, 90
Ford, Henry, 38
Fort Meyers, FL, 28
Ft. Pierce Chronicle, 109

Gainesville, FL, 101
García Márquez, Gabriel: *One Hundred Years of Solitude,* 41
Garifuna people, 4-5, 12, 17, 52, 58, 111
Garrick, Barbara, 39
Gates, Henry Louis, Jr., 5
Gibson, Theodore, 102
Girls Trip (film), 39
Gomez, Samuel, 106, 107
Gonzalez, Jesus, 79
Go Tell It on the Mountain (Baldwin), 113
guajiros (people living in the countryside), 74
Guatemala, xiii, 5, 67

Meyer, Annie Nathan, 135n49
Miami, FL: beauty of, 91; founding of, 92; hotels of, 93; inequalities of, 93; on map, *90*; population of, 89, 93, 99; tourists in, 92–93
Miami Herald, 104, 106
Middle East: Western travellers in, 66
Milne, Alexander, 83–84
Miranda, Carmen, 39
Miskito people, 4, 58
Mitchell, Burroughs, 3, 6, 89, 98
Mobile, AL, 28, 71
Moe, Henry Allen, 32
Mollá, Jordi, 97
Moseley, Harriet, xiv
Moses, Man of the Mountain (Hurston), 133n115
Mosquito Coast: exploration of, 57; Indigenous population of, 58; landscape of, 17, 55, 79; map of, *67*; Mayan ruin on, 81; traditional plants of, 57–58; travels in, 66
Mosquito Coast, The (television series), 57
Moylan, Virginia, xii
mulattoes, 14, 15, 71, 73
Mule Bone: A Comedy of Negro Life (Hughes and Hurston), xiii, 23, 24, 25
mules: as mean of transportation, 60, 65, 75, 76
Mules and Men (Hurston), 106, 132n115, 146n96
Munroe, Ralph, 92
My Lai Massacre, 99, 101

National Association for the Advancement of Colored People (NAACP), 73, 102, 134n17
National Urban League, 112
Negro Digest, 20
Negro Film Institute, 48
New York, NY: civil disturbances in, 19
Nicaragua, 5, 97; civil war in, xiii; map of, *67*; US policy in, 43; war on Honduras, 111–12
"Niggerati," 47
9/11 terrorist attack, 96
Nixon, Richard, 4
Non-Partisan Council, 134n17
Notasulga, AL, 37

O. Henry (William Sydney Porter), 35, 75; on "banana republic," 8–9; *Cabbages and Kings,* 8, 10; trip to Honduras, 8, 9, 129n38
Okeechobee Lake, 28
Olancho departments of Honduras, 59
Olmec people, 56
Omoa, Honduras, 8, 84
Onassis, Jackie, 113
One Hundred Years of Solitude (García Márquez), 41
One Night in Miami (film), 93, 148n29

Panama Canal, 16, 26
Paramount Pictures Corporation, 45, 48, 107
Parrott, Joseph, 92
Patrick Air Force Base, 26
Patuca River, 127n9
Pepper, Claude, 94–95, 98
Perkins, Max, 3, 4
Petry, Ann, 47
Picquet, Louisa, 71–72, 81
Pitt, William, 57
Pitts, James, 26–27
Pittsburgh Courier, 47, 108
Polk County (play), 135n45
Pope, William, 78, 79, 80, 81
Potrerillos, Honduras, 79
Potter, Eliza, 81; *A Hairdresser's Experience in High Life,* 71
Potts, John, 57
Powell, Adam Clayton, Jr., 87
Preston, Andrew, 36–37
Price, Albert, 27
Puerto Cortés, Honduras: Black population of, 4–5; British consul residence in, 80; cost of hotel rooms in, 4; diseases, 4; Hurston's travels to, 79, 81, 82, 117; incident with American military officer, 14–15; labor gangs in, 12; mail service in, 11; postcard with view of, 111–12; rail station, 80; Soltera's visit to, 66
Putnam, Lara, 42

Randolph, A. Philip, 46
Rawlings, Marjorie, 26, 28, 29, 54, 99
Reed, Harrison, 101
Reynolds, Grant, 87